Salt-Water Fishes for the
Home Aquarium

SALT-WATER
FISHES
for the
HOME AQUARIUM

By HELEN SIMKATIS

J. B. LIPPINCOTT COMPANY

PHILADELPHIA & NEW YORK

597
S

74128

I wish to thank the following people for their willingness to take time out of their busy lives to help me when I called upon them for various kinds of assistance. The information they gave me was often highly specialized and not readily available. Mrs. Ida K. Johnson, Librarian, U. S. Fish and Wildlife Service; Dr. F. J. Wood, Curator, Marine Studios, Marineland, Florida; Robert P. Dempster, Associate Curator of Aquatic Biology Steinhart Aquarium, San Francisco; Walter H. Chute, Director, John G. Shedd Aquarium; Francesca LaMonte, Associate Curator of Fishes, The American Museum of Natural History, New York City; William S. Chambers, Jr., Director, Public Relations Marine Studios, Marineland, Florida; Dr. Leonard P. Schultz, Curator of Fishes, U.S. National Museum, Smithsonian Institution; Dr. S. F. Snieszko, Bacteriologist, U.S. Fish and Wildlife Service.

I also wish to express my thanks to Dr. John H. Welsh, Biological Laboratories, Harvard University, and Mr. William S. Chambers, Jr., Marine Studios, Marineland, Florida, for the use of photographs. Drawings by George Simkatis.

CONTENTS

PART ONE

SALT-WATER AQUARIUM
MANAGEMENT

CHAPTER 1

An Introduction to the Marine Fish Hobby

FOR DECADES ichthyologists have been aware of the singularly beautiful salt-water fishes which inhabit the reefs of tropical waters, but only recently have they been brought to the attention of the average aquarist.

Of course, marine tropicals have for many years been displayed in the more ambitious of the public aquariums both in this country and abroad. These institutions obtained their specimens from scientists who from time to time made expeditions to tropical waters and collected fishes for this and other purposes. In these instances, transportation other than commercial was counted on and the fishes were shipped under careful supervision. The curators who received these prizes treated them as highly specialized specimens which, of course, they were. Although papers were written on their maintenance, these accounts were published only in scientific journals not easily accessible to the hobbyist.

The neglect of the marine tropical fish hobby has been the result of a series of factors. One of these is simply that aquarists have been kept busy with fresh-water fishes and on the whole have been willing, until recently, to leave marine tropicals to the professionals. This is understandable because the fresh-water hobby has never been allowed to become static. The aquarist's interests have been stimulated by the new fresh-water fishes that are frequently being introduced as aquarium specimens. In addition, remarkable variations of well-known species are constantly being developed through careful selection and breeding.

As recently as five years ago whatever interest an occasional aquarist might have had in salt-water fishes was inhibited by their inaccessibility, by the persistent rumor that they are difficult to keep alive, and by a lack of data on them.

These factors, among others, were also obstacles from the dealer's point of view. Because the fishes are geographically remote from the crossroads of civilization, perishable in transit, and impossible to keep in tanks designed solely for fresh-water fishes, marine specimens represented a serious financial risk to the businessman.

Furthermore, the dealer was forced to consider the question of salt water. Even if he had a ready source of fishes, he would also, in most instances, have to supply water to his customers. Although the ocean covers almost three-fourths of the earth's surface, sea water becomes an expensive commodity when it has to be shipped even a short distance, and the merchant had to consider this as well as the cost of suitable containers, the expense of shipping and the matter of storage.

These hazards to even the most promising enterprise were too much for the average shop owner. He had security in the familiar fresh-water hobby and there was seemingly no advantage in whetting the appetites of his avid aquarist customers for the exotic salt-water tropicals when they were already quite happy in the fresh-water field.

Perhaps World War II had much to do with bringing marine tropicals to the foreground for, during that period, many aquarists traveled more extensively than ever before. Those who were sent to the tropics discovered for the first time the beautiful salt-water specimens indigenous to warm waters and became intrigued with the prospect of taking collections home to be included in their own aquariums.

After the war people continued to travel, more so than during any other peacetime period in history. They returned to places that had attracted them during the war or else they were inspired to visit places about which they had read.

Resorts and large cities attracted thousands of people who took to the road. As aquariums are listed in the guidebooks among the things to see, these institutions were besieged by eager tourists among whom were, of course, a good number of aquarists. Certainly aquariums such as the Shedd in Chicago, the Steinhart in San Francisco, and Marine Studios, the oceanarium in Florida, all of which display marine tropicals, have had important roles in converting many a fresh-water hobbyist to the salt-water field.

Shortly after the war, occasional shipments of perhaps two or three salt-water specimens each would reach the more progressive dealers. When the word got around among the customers of such a dealer, the shipment was treated as a great event and they all trooped to the fortunate fellow's shop to gaze into his tank at the small exotic arrivals. The dealer himself was awed by the beauty of the little fellows but his grim hope was that his customers would take home enough black mollies or red swordtails to warrant his outlay for them. The prices of salt-water tropicals in those days were enough to stop the average aquarist from doing more than look and, of course, not even the most progressive dealers were properly equipped to handle them. A few die-hard aquarists would go home and secretly add up a few figures. A day or two later, after much thought (but without consulting their respective spouses) they would return to the dealer's shop, ready to buy, only to learn that the exotics had died that morning.

The small salt-water fishes would become but a lovely memory to the aquarists who had been lucky enough to see them, and no more than a tax deduction to the dealer. The aquarist, in his more exalted moments, may recall these brilliantly hued little creatures and then begin to wonder where . . . how . . .?

To the uninitiated, this may seem an odd way to spend an exalted moment, but then the aquarist is himself an odd and elusive fish. He may be young or old, Republican or Democrat; he may be and very often is *she;* he may be doctor or laborer; he may be discovered in any financial bracket. Regardless of these and other differences, however, we can sum him up by saying that he is mentally still growing, for he has imagination and intellectual curiosity; that he loves living things, admires the beautiful, and, in most cases, is really a very nice Joe (or Josephine).

So, if we followed our particular aquarist a little further, we would find him searching the shelves of the biology section of his library. Later we'd see him consulting his bankbook, later his boss, and last of all his wife. Because he lives in a northeastern section of the country, he would have found that the waters off southern Florida were his closest source of marine tropical fishes, and his next step would be to convince his wife that southern Florida, after all, is *the* vacation spot of the nation. She, of necessity, being a sympathetic spouse and tolerant soul, would agree and ask brightly, "When do we start?" From there on our persistent fellow would be on his own.

If he lives in the northwestern section of the United States, he may have chosen the southern shores of California as his collecting grounds. For that matter the coastal waters of any area are rich in interesting marine life, but the most colorful species of fishes are confined to southern waters.

During the late 'forties a number of avid aquarists must have considered the prospect of collecting marine tropicals, for about that time brief accounts of such ventures began to appear in the various aquarium magazines.

It is difficult to track down a trend but in 1948 the number of aquarists interested in the marine hobby was certainly comparatively modest. Then in 1950 a large aquarium firm in New York advertised a mixture of artificial salts that would, when dissolved in tap water and added to a fusion of natural sea water, support small marine animals. In addition, the firm sent out exciting lists of marine fishes at comparatively low prices. These were the first indications that the marine hobby was beginning to grow into a commercial enterprise. New words and expressions were creeping into conversations between aquarists but at this time the only book we were able to find on the subject in dealers' stores was a pamphlet written by Bernard Gardner. Brief as the work was, Mr. Gardner crammed much information into it and had apparently done considerable research in its preparation. The marine aquarist who found it on his dealer's shelf was indeed fortunate, for it pointed out some of the basic rules for marine aquarium maintenance and noted some of the difficulties involved in the pursuit. Mr. Gardner, in his conclusion, promised a more complete book on the subject, but his untimely death prevented this.

Although the marine hobby was extremely attractive and seemed to offer great rewards, it was at this point a kind of will-o'-the-wisp that enticed a fellow into spending too much money and energy for that inevitable tank of dead fishes. Well-informed collectors, shippers, and dealers were still a rarity. There were many obstacles in the way of the salt-water aquarist.

After a while the large aquarium company in New York stopped talking about marine fishes. The advertisements for their salts disappeared and their list of salt-water specimens was no longer circulated in the mail. We can only guess that the owner of this establishment began to add up the cost and then shook his head doubtfully. The collectors he was dealing with were at best ill-informed on shipping methods, the best yet to be developed. Aquarium equipment was still designed for the fresh-water trade only, air freight was prohibitive in cost and, worst of all, the fishes often died in transit (at the dealer's expense) or before they were sold. If they didn't die on the dealer's hands, they soon perished in his customer's tank, which was just as bad in the long run. Another important factor was that even when fishes were available, aquarists willing to take the necessary risks were few. Although there was undoubtedly a flare of interest in the field, it was feeble and not enough missionary work had been done to keep it alive. At this time it seemed that the hobby had taken its last breath.

However, we must never forget the die-hards. We knew several of these persistent fellows and worked very close to one in particular. Because he opened up such a wonderfully colorful and interesting world to us, we have dedicated this book to him.

He was one of the aquarists we mentioned earlier—one of those who trooped down to see a shipment of exotic marine tropical fishes a dealer had chanced to receive. And, of course, he was one of those who went home and quietly added up a few figures, but before he had a chance to purchase any of the rare, little brightly colored scraps of marine life, they had died. Disappointed, he returned home and wondered why.

He consulted books and maps and more books. He drove thousands of miles and lugged hundreds of gallons of water. He overcame his fear of sharks and collected many specimens in tropical waters and set up many a marine aquarium. We've known him to collect water in north-eastern Atlantic waters in January because the water in his aquarium was questionable and his specimens were not behaving up to par. He waded cheerfully in icy waters, filling his large glass jugs in an incoming tide and, bucking the icy wind, lugged them to his car. He did all of these things many times before he learned any of the answers. For the most part, his was a trial and error method, a process that took much time and energy, especially since our friend had digested much of the inaccurate information generally accepted at that time.

He still doesn't know all the answers, but he has learned enough to assure himself that he can set up a tank and be reasonably sure of what's happening inside it. He knows what he can and cannot use in his aquarium and how to provide his colorful marine beauties with a fairly reasonable facsimile of the reef life to which they are accustomed. In those days, however, he and a mere handful of other die-hards were working alone in the face of failures made by groups that were far better equipped and financed than they for such experimentation.

One other encouraging aspect in the hobby at that time was the fact that the editors of the aquarium magazines were willing to publish articles on the findings of these hardy souls. Such pieces appeared from time to time and very often were filled with invaluable information for the newly initiated who would otherwise have been working completely alone.

We have told you much about the persistent aquarist but there were also dealers who were die-hards. Within recent years there have been a few who have shown a reluctance to give up the idea of marine fishes for the home aquarium despite the fact that the venture entailed much risk and demanded much missionary work. They have done much toward teaching their customers the art of keeping marine fishes in closed-system aquariums. Among these are Kay and William Jue of Mei Lan in Oakland, California. Mr. and Mrs. Jue have developed dry foods and medications which have been successfully used in the salt-water hobby. Jon Groetzinger of White Plains, New York (Westchester Aquarium Supply Company), also has been active in the field. He has contributed an important forward stride by introducing a mixture of salts that produces an artificial sea water when dissolved in tap water. Although similar products had appeared before, Mr. Groetzinger's faith in his own product has helped make his venture a successful one. He has devoted much time to publicizing his formula and the marine hobby along with it. He has brought marine fishes into the living rooms of people who live many miles inland through the medium of television. The work involved in setting up such programs is awesome when one considers the hauling of tanks, the mixing of water, as well as the securing and maintaining of specimens. He put on one of the largest salt-water shows ever attempted in a well-known New York department store. His formula opened up the hobby to thousands of aquarists who couldn't have attempted it before because of the difficulty involved in securing salt water. Pounds of the salts were shipped to inlanders and dealers began to stock the product all over the country. No longer was a dealer confronted with the problem of the storage of water. He could now offer marine fishes to his customers and have artificial salts on hand to go along with them.

Soon after Mr. Groetzinger's artificial salt-water mix appeared on the market, other dealers and manufacturers offered similar formulas. Manufacturers began to design aquarium equipment with the marine hobby in mind and little by little what had been a hobby for only a few was becoming the pursuit of many. Many seemingly insurmountable problems were being solved.

Timing is an important factor in the success of any venture. Although a great deal of the publicity the hobby received at first was due to Mr. Groetzinger's efforts, interest was generated from many different sources. The introduction of the aqualung and other underwater-breathing apparatus which promoted skin diving as a sport played a part in the hobby. Newspaper and magazine articles on marine life began to appear and even people who were unfamiliar with the already firmly established fresh-water field became fascinated by the prospect of keeping the colorful reef fishes in their homes. Hollywood entered into the spirit of the new interest by producing short features and full-length movies that were related to marine subjects. Rachael Carson's *The Sea Around Us* was one of the better films offered. Accounts of longevity records began to appear in the aquarium magazines and conservatives in the fresh-water field who had thought the marine fish hobby was merely a fad, began to change their tune.

Gradually the obstacles that confronted the marine hobbyists began to melt away. One of the most important steps was the abandonment of the old system of transporting fishes. The German shipping can, a familiar object to aquarists for years, was set aside for the new plastic shipping bag. The can had been useful in that it was insurance against breakage and leakage. Its sloping sides allowed for a haphazard kind of aeration during the in-transit time, but it had to be supplemented with a chemical compound to insure adequate aeration.

The plastic bag proved far more versatile for many reasons. Its lighter weight reduced shipping costs and it lent itself to a very efficient method of aeration. Simply by partially inflating the part of the bag not filled with water with oxygen under pressure and tying the top of the bag securely, many more fishes could be delivered at one time without any losses due to lack of oxygen. In the marine hobby this method was important for another reason. Metals and salt water do not make a happy combination under any circumstances but plastic does not break down chemically when in contact with salt water. Salt-water fishes have been flown successfully more than halfway around the world in plastic bags. Such long trips would have been impossible had cans been used as containers.

There is room for improvement in many aspects of the hobby, but because some of the greatest of the difficulties have been satisfactorily removed, we are assured that the remaining ones will be ironed out eventually. The pioneering still to be done in the field offers a challenge.

More and more, beautiful species have been coming into the country, but only a sample of the kinds of salt-water fishes that are adaptable to home aquariums have been seen by the most advanced aquarists. Because of the increased demand, the cost of specimens has gone down considerably. However, the process of catching a fish and eventually getting it into the aquarium of the hobbyist in a healthy condition involves a great deal of teamwork. The number of people with specialized knowledge necessary to complete a shipment of fishes from Africa, Hawaii, or even from our own Florida Keys, is a little frightening.

To begin with, the collector must be aware of the exigencies of his business. In foreign countries, the collector works for a shipper and is only one of many employed in this capacity. The shipper of necessity has learned the business of preparing fishes for shipment. Collectors in our own country, however, are playing a new and different role. In addition to knowing their business as collector, they must learn how to prepare shipments. Furthermore they should know how to handle and care for the specimens they gather, as they may have to hold the fishes for some days before shipping time. In the early days, when orders were few and far between, the purchaser usually took care of the shipping himself by issuing detailed instructions or by being on the spot when the collector came into dock. Rarely was the collector required to hold his specimens for any appreciable time. If he didn't have an order, he simply didn't collect any fish. Now the specimens he collects and holds are like money in the bank. If he hasn't an order today, he's bound to have a large one tomorrow. The collector has become businessman, aquarist and shipper.

As the industry grows, his position will probably become similar to that of the foreign shipper and he will have many collectors working for him. At present, however, a collector often catches his own stock, advertises, and sells. In order to be good at his job, he has to take time out to learn his trade. The specimens he collects today may later become part of a large shipment that is slated for a dealer fifteen hundred miles away, to be sent out tomorrow or a week from tomorrow. Such specimens have to be handled gently from the moment they are caught for even today, with shipping methods greatly improved, fishes go through much hardship during their journey. If they are kept on the collector's premises for any length of time, they must be nourished and rested in proper tanks, and in uncontaminated water. If these matters aren't carefully considered, the specimens will arrive at their destination in bad condition. The dealer on the receiving end may not complain at first but if fishes continue to arrive in bad shape, he is bound to take his business elsewhere. The collector is now participating in one branch of a hobby that earns millions of dollars every year in this country. To be successful he must learn new methods. If he tells himself he has been collecting for twenty years and that there is nothing in the business he doesn't know, he's only fooling himself; the people with whom he is dealing will not be so gullible.

The dealers, too, are going through a period of acquiring new knowledge. No matter how proficient the collector and shipper are, all is lost if the fishes are handled poorly after their arrival. The dealer must learn a great deal about the art of salt-water aquarium maintenance, not only for the more obvious reasons, but also because he is often the only source of information the aquarist may have. Of course, the aquarist who consults his library and periodicals has the advantage of enriching his know-how from many sources. Unfortunately, a great many hobbyists go no further than their dealer's store for information. We know of one dealer who opened a shop in a new suburban area where the people were completely uninitiated in the hobby. He painstakingly answered their questions, going over every step with each individual who asked for help. Eventually, he stimulated great interest in his area and created a first-class base of operations. His store flourished and his customers became skilled under his guidance. Such a role demands, first of all, sound knowledge and, later, the ability to get it across. So, if the collector must know his trade as well as being aquarist and businessman, the dealer must be all of these and one more—a patient and willing teacher.

The aquarist is the last, but far from the least important, member on this team. Until recently he has been working against great odds. The paucity of written material on the marine fish hobby has been appalling. The articles that have come to us through magazines devoted to tropical fishes are often thoughtfully written but usually cover only one phase of the salt-water hobby. Often they are based on a single experience and do not represent any accumulation of work and study.

However, because of innovations, inventions and, most of all, because many people have been thinking and working together on the problems involved in marine aquarium maintenance, much of the risk in the hobby has been reduced. When a demand is created in volume for anything, there is usually an inventive mind that comes up with a way to supply it. The water problem, for example, is going through the mental mills of the creative people in the field. New formulas for salt water are being developed and easily handled concentrates are being placed on the market; ways and means to reduce transportation costs are constantly being considered and presented. Although the results of study of marine animals in captivity are still not coming through to hobbyists as fast as could be desired, enough information has been presented to encourage the manufacture of equipment necessary to the hobby. Drugs have been developed that allow shippers the advantage of sending more fishes longer distances with fewer deaths of specimens occurring during the in-transit time. As a result of all these developments, the collector has a job, the dealer has a source, and the aquarist has a fish, along with the assurance that he can keep it in his tank for a satisfactory length of time.

We have had many interesting letters from aquarists all over the world who have achieved success in the salt-water hobby. In these reports we have been surprised by the variety of methods of approach employed. In every case, however, certain hard and fixed rules have been followed. This book is based on the methods behind these experiments, our own, and the findings of scientists who are devoted to highly specialized phases of the study of fishes. We have tried to organize our material in a way that will enable the hobbyist to have information at his finger tips when he needs it.

Sometimes we are asked why anyone should want to bother with salt-water specimens at all when the fresh-water field is so interesting, uninvolved, and neatly packaged. We point out, of course, that it wasn't too long ago that the fresh-water hobby was suffering from growing pains and we should give a respectful thought to those who expended the time and effort to produce such a neat package. This is not, however, the best defense of the present interest in salt-water fishes.

The strongest point in favor of marine specimens is their almost unbelievable beauty. If a blue is present in a fresh-water fish, the color often depends on lighting to bring it out. A salt-water fish has its vivid coloring regardless of lighting conditions. The reef fishes encompass the spectrum; no other creatures in nature are painted more extravagantly than these. And if the philosopher reminds us at this point that beauty is superficial, we hasten to reply that salt-water fishes have character and personality to add to their loveliness. They tame very quickly in captivity and they learn rapidly. A lift of a finger and they are performing brilliant choreographies in colors that would dazzle the most blasé of ballet audiences. Each variety is demonstrating in its inimitable way that a tidbit would be welcome. No request could be expressed more eloquently.

We might point out, too, that salt-water fishes under good conditions are long-lived. One of the most beautiful of the exotics, the *Amphiprion percula*, or clownfish, has lived for seven years in a closed-system aquarium. A sea anemone could very well outlive its owner.

We hope this book will introduce a bright and fascinating new interest to those who are unfamiliar with the salt-water tropicals and will enable those already aware of the various beautiful forms of marine life to enjoy fully the rich rewards that can be derived from a hobby that is at once challenging, stimulating and satisfying.

CHAPTER 2

Setting Up the Salt-Water Aquarium

*Choosing the Aquarium • Filtration and Aera-
tion • Other Necessary Equipment • Ornaments
and Decor • Selection of Specimens and Pointers
on Ordering Them • Miscellaneous Specimens
Offered by Dealers • Installing the Salt-Water
Aquarium • Introducing Specimens to Their
New Home • Marine Aquarium Management.*

Choosing the Aquarium

THE preliminaries of setting up a salt-water aquarium include,
among other pertinent considerations, the selection of the types of
equipment compatible with the hobby. We will not discuss here in detail the underlying reasons for the suggestions that follow, as each
phase and idiosyncrasy of the pursuit will be considered in later
chapters.

The selection of the type of tank you want will be your first major
decision. The variety of tanks that can be used successfully are definitely limited for reasons that will be explained as we go along.

Your aquarium walls will be a barrier between what is perfectly
normal for you and a contrived normalcy for the colorful specimens
you choose for your salt-water pets. You are inviting a bit of the sea
to come into your living room and although you cannot hope to imi-
tate on a diminutive scale the vast complex and exquisitely balanced
aquarium we call the sea, you will attempt to do so. Its esthetic, bio-

logical and chemical make-up must be considered and these characteristics will be maintained as faithfully as possible by whatever means you have at your disposal.

Your tank will be the framework for the animated seascape you are creating, and therefore claims esthetic importance. Its interior will be in constant contact with the aquarium water; therefore, its composition must meet with the necessary standards of chemical stability in order to hold the kind of biological balance that eventually is reached in an established aquarium.

The sea, regardless of how unharnessed it is and no matter how much of the earth's surface it claims, is cradled by the land. The winds that blow across the plains, the rains that fall on the hills and valleys, the heat and cold that strike the land, and, of course, the physical make-up of the earth itself, all affect the biochemistry of the sea.

A somewhat similar relationship will exist between your aquarium and the water in it. If the materials used in the construction of your tank are chemically unstable when they come in contact with salt water, both water and materials will be affected. In this case, it is the change in the water that is critical, for some changes can be lethal to your specimens.

Chemical changes in aquarium water are far more exaggerated proportionately than those that occur in the sea, for although changes go on endlessly in the ocean, they balance and counterbalance each other chemically. It is said that no part of the sea is chemically identical to another. Because of currents and tides sea water is never static, so no concentration of contaminated water from one particular source is ever maintained for very long. The creatures of the sea can, for the most part, adapt to sudden changes in the water, for such alterations are never prevalent for long.

If, however, a really great change occurs in the sea, such as the red tide phenomenon, thousands of fishes perish. The red tide is caused by a sudden stimulation in growth of a certain tiny plant-animal. For reasons still unexplained satisfactorily by science, this microscopic red organism suddenly flourishes, thereby invading vast areas of the water's surface. It cuts off the oxygen supply and is caught in the delicate gills of fishes and strangles even such large sea mammals as porpoises and whales. Even creatures on the floor of the ocean are destroyed by it because their source of oxygen is depleted.

On the other hand, a metal object on the ocean floor does little to upset its surrounding chemical environment for the water around it is not static. We make this point because aquarists often ask why one has to be so fastidious about metal when it has been noted many times that fishes have been found living around the steel skeletons of wrecked ships. Iron salts from such metals are constantly diluted and swept away by the constant motion of the sea. If a comparable object were confined to a man-made pool containing salt water, the situation would be entirely different. Eventually any creatures confined to such a pool would be affected unless they happened to be the kinds of sea animals that enjoy wide tolerances to chemical changes.

Likewise, should a cement used in the construction of an aquarium break down chemically, there is, of course, no tide to sweep away or dilute the contaminated water, nor is there any natural counterbalance for the upset. As time goes on, the change becomes more acute. A toxic condition develops steadily in the tank and, as reef fishes are extremely sensitive to toxicity of any kind, it isn't long before the fishes are lost.

This problem doesn't exist in the comparatively small wall tanks of Marine Studios of Marineland, Florida, because water is constantly pumped into them from the sea. Other great aquariums that depend on a circulating system, however, are extremely cautious to eliminate all possible sources of toxicity because, although water flows through their tanks continuously, they are limited to a large reserve tank of water. In this way they use the same water over and over again. If toxicity were allowed to build up in the reserve, the result would spell disaster.

The aquarist is limited still further because his reserve of water amounts to comparatively few gallons in what is called a closed-system aquarium. Because there is no flow of new water passing through his aquarium it is imperative that his water be kept chemically balanced. Therefore, the first factor to consider when selecting an aquarium is whether or not the materials used in its construction are chemically stable in salt water.

Pioneers in the marine hobby have been experimenting with many different types of tanks. Glass and Plexiglas are both considered reasonably stable materials in salt water. Glass, being the older, has received more scrutiny. Although a slight increase of silicate has been discovered in salt water stored in glass containers, this change has proved harmless to specimens.

A glass aquarium without any metal frame would then be ideal if it could be made large enough. However, molded glass aquariums are not widely used, largely because they are subject to breakage. Bonded glass aquariums have been built to order for aquarists and used successfully; but they are expensive and extreme care must be taken with them to avoid breakage. They must be placed on perfectly smooth surfaces so that their bottoms do not crack as a result of pressure from the water's weight. Their fragility detracts from the assurance they offer otherwise.

Plexiglas tanks have proved completely satisfactory. A tank of this type may be purchased through an aquarium dealer or can be built to order by a fabricator of Plexiglas. If you employ a fabricator to build a tank for you, specify that he use Ethylene Dichloride for bonding. This is a solvent cement that has been used successfully in the manufacture of Plexiglas tanks and appliances designed for salt-water use.

The advantages of using Plexiglas are readily discernible. First of all, the material does not break easily. Some authorities have questioned the use of bonded Plexiglas, but it has been our experience and observation that it is perfectly safe if Ethylene Dichloride is used, as this bonding agent is a solvent to Plexiglas. It fuses the parts together and any excess is lost by evaporation, the Ethylene Dichloride being extremely volatile. A newly constructed tank should not be filled with water immediately. The bonding agent should be given twenty-four hours in which to fuse the parts and allow the excess to dissipate. It should then be filled with fresh water so that any leaks (if present) can be corrected. This is a fairly simple operation.

Some aquarists have objected to Plexiglas because it scratches easily. This can be avoided if care is taken that no abrasive material is used when cleaning the surfaces. Inside scratches, if not too deep, disappear through optical illusion. For a tank of more than ten-gallon capacity, Plexiglas of one-half-inch thickness should be used. Anything thinner will bow in time and ruin the appearance of an otherwise beautiful aquarium. Plexiglas does not discolor with time and requires no maintenance. A stand with a solid top must be used with a plastic tank; one with merely an open frame will not do.

The aquarist has still another choice of aquariums. In recent years reputable manufacturers have been building metal-frame tanks with cements guaranteed to be chemically stable in salt water. Such an aquarium from a reliable manufacturer is a good risk. The price compares favorably with that of a standard tank and it does not have to be made to order. Further, it can be repaired in case a leak develops. The chief disadvantage of such a tank is the fact that one must depend completely on what the manufacturer claims to be a cement chemically stable in salt water. Most manufacturers are reluctant to reveal the ingredients used in the cement formula. Nevertheless, the reports on such tanks have been good. They have been used by aquarists who can show impressive longevity records; that is, by aquarists who have kept individual specimens for substantial periods.

Fiberglas-lined wooden tanks have not, to our knowledge, been successful in closed-system aquariums. Aquariums that are built so that the glass extends above the top metal frame are of no particular value unless their manufacturers have used cement which is chemically stable in salt water.

To summarize briefly, three types of tanks are acceptable. The all-glass aquarium is unquestionably safe chemically but risky because of its fragility. The metal-frame tank, built with chemically stable cement is easily accessible, reasonably priced; the only objection to it is that its use involves the employment of a material the ingredients of which are unknown to you. The Plexiglas tank is chemically safe and is fairly accessible. There are no questionable materials used in its construction, and although it is somewhat more costly than the metal-frame tank, it requires no maintenance, which compensates for its higher price.

When you have decided upon the type of tank you are going to use, you will next want to consider the size best suited for marine specimens, the location you have chosen for your aquarium—and your pocketbook. Salt-water fishes requires more room per fish than do fresh-water varieties. Further, the larger the volume of water, the better the chances of keeping it in good condition. This will be explained in more detail in the chapter on water. We do not recommend a tank with less than a fifteen-gallon capacity. If a larger one is feasible, you should by all means get one. It is far better to invest in a large tank when first going into the hobby than to scrimp on it in order to purchase more fishes. The novice aquarist should limit the number of specimens he buys anyway. You can increase your aquarium family later when you have developed your skill. Only then will you fully appreciate that a small aquarium is not a good investment.

You will probably want to purchase a lighting fixture with your tank. No matter what kind of tank light you select, you should plan to place it over a glass so that any metal surface will not be exposed to the condensation of the water from your aquarium. All types of contact between water and metal should be avoided. Without a glass the condensation would collect on the metal of the lighting fixture and eventually drip back into the tank, carrying metal salts with it which, as we have explained previously, are deleterious to marine life.

Fluorescent lights are advised if a Plexiglas tank is your choice; these lights give off less heat than incandescent bulbs. Plexiglas softens when exposed to high temperatures and although the incandescent bulbs would not necessarily produce temperatures high enough to be dangerous, the fluorescent type is a good deal safer. This suggestion would also apply if an all-glass tank has been selected.

If your tank is to be placed in a corner of your home where there is little or no daylight, almost all the photosynthesis that takes place in your aquarium will depend upon the artificial lighting you supply. Incandescent light is more efficient under those conditions, but whether you use incandescent or fluorescent lighting, photosynthetic action will be feeble if you depend solely on artificial lighting. However weak this action is, it will be of some benefit. We will discuss this question more thoroughly in the chapter devoted to water.

When purchasing fluorescent tubes, select the daylight type and if these are to be the only source of light, two 30-watt tubes, or one 60-watt tube should be used.

Filtration and Aeration

Filtration and aeration are your next considerations. Both functions are very important in the salt-water aquarium and the equipment you select to perform them should be appraised most carefully.

A wide variety of pumps and accessories are available and probably none of them is entirely without merit. As the salt-water hobby demands a great degree of efficiency in the methods of aeration and filtration employed, it might be well to examine rather closely the various types available.

The standard method of aeration requires an electric-motor-driven air pump. Air is pushed through flexible plastic tubing into the aquarium water. A number of aquariums can be serviced from such a pump by the addition of a tee connection at each point in the line where a supply of air is necessary. When the air is released into the water, it is dispersed by an airstone that fits on the line. A spray of bubbles forms and since these are lighter than water, they spring up to the surface and break. On the upward journey, some oxygen dissolves into the water. However, their most important function is to cause a light current which is instrumental in allowing the free carbon dioxide in the water to escape.

Filtration by the standard method is also accomplished with the use of an electric-motor-driven air pump. Water is drawn up through a tube by an airlift and is released into a filter chamber. Here waste material is caught by the filtering material and the water passes through back to the aquarium (*see* Figure 1). The same electric-motor-driven air pump serves both the air line and the filtering system. There are many variations of the standard method of aeration and filtration but they all work more or less on the same principle.

Care should be taken, if the standard method of aeration is employed, that spray from the breaking bubbles does not come in contact with the inner side of the top metal frame. The filtering medium should be cleaned fairly often so that solid excrement is washed away along with other waste materials. Charcoal serves no good purpose in the salt-water tank unless it is changed constantly, since it becomes a source of soluble waste products once it has been saturated with them. In addition, the processing of charcoal by the manufacturer is an un-

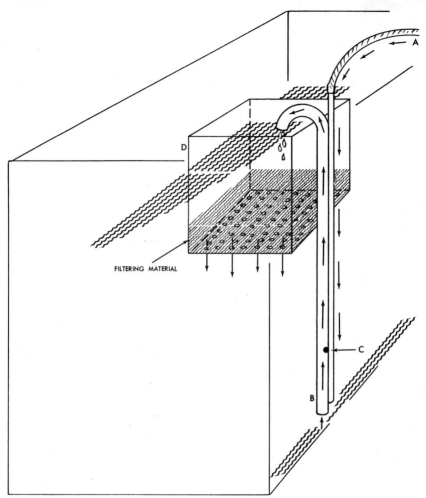

Figure 1. STANDARD FILTER

A Air line; **B** Water-lift tube and air tube bonded together except where water-lift tube curves over filter box (**D**); **C** Dot indicates where perforations in both tubes of **B** meet; **D** Filter box.

Air moves from **A** (air line) into the air tube of **B**. As this tube is sealed at the bottom, the air is forced through **C** (meeting perforations of both tubes). Water, which has entered into the water-lifting tube which is not sealed at the bottom, is lifted by the forced air and is pushed up as the arrows indicate until it escapes and drops down into **D** (filter box). Particles in it are caught by the filtering material in the box and clean water is returned to the aquarium.

31

known factor; for that reason alone, its use is debatable. Glass wool can be used but care should be taken that bits of it are not broken off to become suspended in the aquarium water. The chances of this are slight with the standard method of filtration described above. Nevertheless, there is the possibility that such suspended material could become entangled in the delicate filaments of the gills of the fishes, causing their death. A far better medium has recently become available to aquarists. It is a napped nylon material, loosely woven and undyed, and can be purchased from your dealer or from the yard-goods counter of your department store. It is about as thick as the average blanket and is made of one hundred per cent nylon which is chemically stable in salt water. It can be washed out and used many times. It is especially useful in catching brown algae that grow profusely in the aquarium water at times. If you purchase this material at your department store, make sure it is marked one hundred per cent nylon. A half yard will serve you a long time. Cut it into pieces that will fit comfortably in your filter box. Only one thickness need be used. It might be a good idea to rinse the pad before placing it in the box to remove any sizing that may be present.

Another type of filtration that has become popular in recent years is described as biological filtration. Although there are various modifications of this system available, they all work on the same principle. A perforated plastic plate is placed on the floor of the tank (see Figure 2) and sand is poured over it. A water-lifting tube fits into a neck present on the plate. The aquarium water slowly filters through the layer of sand which is from two to three inches deep. After it passes through the perforations in the plate supporting the sand, it rises up the water-lifting tube and is released once more into the aquarium. The theory behind this system is that waste material is caught in the sand where beneficial bacteria reduce it to plant nutrients. As it is processed in this manner, algae and plants absorb it. A biological balance is supposedly maintained among the various bacteria so that no particular kind thrives over the others. This type of filtration may prove successful in fresh-water aquariums where rooted plants are present. Vegetation may become luxuriant with such a system and the gravel appear remarkably clean. In the salt-water aquarium, however, the only plants ever used are the algal forms. Algae do not receive nourishment

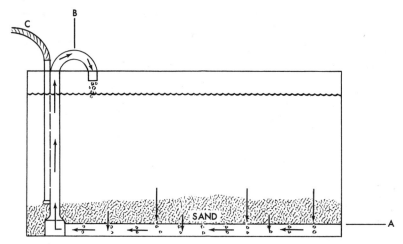

Figure 2. THE SUB-SAND FILTER OR BIOLOGICAL FILTER

A Perforated or slotted plate; **B** Water-lift tube and air tube bonded together except where water-lift tube curves over interior of aquarium; **C** Air line.

A (a perforated or slotted plate) fits on the floor of the aquarium. It is raised about an inch above the floor of the tank. Water-lift tube of **B** fits into neck on the plate. **B** in this filtering device functions in the same way as does **B** of Figure 1. A layer of sand is poured over **A** (perforated or slotted plate) to a depth of from two to three inches. The tank is then filled with water. The aquarium water filters through the sand and perforations in the plate. The filtered water that fills the space between the floor of the tank and the plate is lifted up the water-lift tube as the arrows in the drawing indicate and is returned to the aquarium. A constant but slow circulation of water is thus achieved.

through roots, so such an accumulation of waste would be of no particular advantage in the marine aquarium. Furthermore, only a thin layer of sand is advocated, as a thick mass would make for the very conditions we are trying to avoid, that is, a low bacteria count, and, as no rooted plants are ever present in the marine aquarium, deep sand serves no purpose whatsoever. One expert suggests that a vacuum-cleaner type of device be improvised to collect waste directly from the floor of the tank, thus preventing excrement from contacting the water on its upward journey to the surface. He is of the opinion that the less excrement allowed to come in contact with the aquarium water and allowed to remain in it, the easier it will be to keep salt water in a healthy condition. Even though we do not believe it is pos-

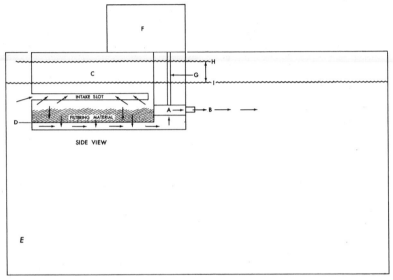

Figure 3. THE POWER FILTER

A Impeller; **B** Opening for jetted water; **C** Filter box; **D** Slotted plate; **E** Aquarium; **F** Motor housing; **G** Shaft; **H** and **I** The highest and lowest points respectively that the water line in the tank can be.

A (impeller) spins around in a chamber with an opening on side (**B**). Impeller chamber is backed by **C** (filter box) which is slotted on three sides so that water flows into it from the aquarium as arrows in drawing indicate. The side adjacent to impeller chamber is closed. **D** (slotted plate) rests about an inch above the bottom of the filter box (**C**). Filtering material is placed on **D** and water flowing in from the aquarium filters through it. The filtered water in the space between **D** and the bottom of **C** is sucked out by the spinning impeller (**A**) and jetted out through **B,** causing a current in the aquarium water. A fast circulation of water is accomplished (some power filters filter water at the rate of 100 gallons per hour).

sible or necessary to keep the aquarium this free of waste products, we feel that any system that allows quantities of waste material to accumulate is dangerous. Some bacterial action is taking place in the salt-water aquarium that is not equipped with a sub-sand filter, for it would be impossible to keep a tank free of such tiny forms of life, and the algae that grow on the walls of the aquarium do benefit somewhat from waste products that are converted by bacterial action into plant nutrients, but all of this material is not utilized. The aquarist welcomes whatever biological balance that may exist in his aquarium but he realizes that it would be of no advantage to allow the bacteria count to increase.

The most efficient filtering and aerating device available for the marine aquarist is the power filter. It consists of an electric-motor-driven impeller that spins around in a chamber that has an opening on one side. A filter chamber backs the impeller compartment and allows the water to flow into it by intake holes (*see* Figures 3 and 4). A nylon pad or layer of glass wool is placed over a plate in the filter chamber and the water is drawn through this material to the area under it. The spinning impeller sucks this filtered water out and it is jetted into the aquarium proper at a rapid rate. Thus a current is

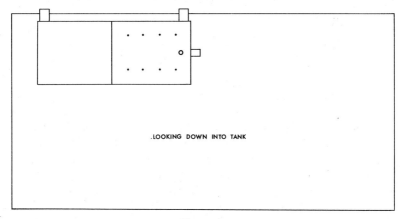

.LOOKING DOWN INTO TANK

Figure 4.

Position power filter takes in tank (looking down into aquarium).

created. New surfaces of water meet the air constantly and are charged with oxygen. At the same time the free carbon dioxide in the water escapes. This power-driven device thereby aerates, circulates and filters the aquarium water. Some makes circulate the water through the filtering material at the rate of approximately one hundred gallons per hour. The current is beneficial, too, in that it provides the fishes with exercise; in effect, it acts somewhat like a race wheel in a squirrel cage. Of course, there are quiet spots in the tank so that no fish need swim in the rapidly moving water unless it chooses to do so.

The power filter is more costly than the standard setup as it will service only one tank at a time. An electric timer should be used in conjunction with it so that the current is turned on an hour and off an hour all around the clock automatically. The hour in which the pump is quiet affords the fishes a resting period without causing them to suffer from lack of air. There are electric timers on the market that will maintain a twenty-four-hour program without resetting. One timer will service a number of pumps or other electric appliances.

To summarize the aeration and filtering methods we have described, we might class the standard method as the most economical, the power filter the most efficient, and the biological or sub-sand filters as undesirable in the salt-water aquarium. The standard method employs one air pump which may service a number of aquariums. None of these, however, will be aerated or filtered as efficiently as an aquarium serviced by a power filter that pulls water through filtering material at the rate of one hundred gallons per hour. The make of power-filter should be considered carefully before purchase is made, as some brands employ metal shafts and impellers. As these parts are exposed to the aquarium water, they should be made of plastic. Stainless steel is not acceptable as it is not impervious to salt water. If the power filter is used only occasionally as a filtering device, standard aeration, of course will be necessary. Many aquarists move a power filter from one aquarium to another, using it wherever it is needed to clear up cloudy water or to remove insoluble waste. Although the power filter is a handy appliance for this type of duty, the aquarist who uses it in conjunction with an electric timer so that it runs intermittently day and night, servicing one aquarium only, is getting the most out of a very efficient piece of equipment.

Other Necessary Equipment

Glass wool has been the accepted filtering material for a number of years and because it is chemically inert in salt water, it has been used by marine aquarists also. Under close scrutiny, however, many serious aquarists have agreed recently that the use of glass wool might well be discontinued in view of the efficiency offered by new products that are easier to handle. The complaint expressed most frequently against the use of glass wool is its tendency to break off in tiny particles when handling and when in use in the aquarium. Several new products have been made available recently that are as efficient as glass wool without possessing its bad features. One of these is the napped nylon material mentioned previously in this chapter. This useful material is inert in salt water, does a very fine filtering job, can be washed out very easily and used over again many times, and can be cut to fit any filter box. A nylon staple has been introduced also, which is the nylon yarn or unwoven material. Although it is easier to handle than glass wool and does not impregnate the aquarium water with tiny fibers, it is apt to become too impacted in the filter box after it is used for any length of time, and is difficult to wash out properly. Sponges consisting of vinyl plastic can be used but these, like the nylon staple material, are difficult to wash out satisfactorily.

Along with a reliable thermometer, the aquarist should own a hydrometer. This instrument will be discussed more thoroughly in the chapter on water. It is designed to measure the density or salinity of salt water. Density or salinity can be controlled by the addition of salt or fresh water, whichever the hydrometer indicates is necessary. As 1.025 is the hydrometric reading of water collected off the Florida Keys, this reading should be included in the range covered by the hydrometer the aquarist elects to purchase. As the temperature of the water affects the reading, a hydrometer designed for 70° would be ideal. As most hydrometers are designed for 60° Fahrenheit, however, one of these can be used. How to make the necessary correction will be explained in Chapter 3, in the section on salinity control.

A thermostatically controlled heater is desirable for the salt-water aquarium. Be sure that if the clip or hanger on the make you select comes in contact with the water that it is made of plastic. The heater should be set to maintain a temperature from 70° to 74° Fahrenheit. During winter nights, when people lower the thermostats that regulate their furnaces, a thermostatically controlled heater will assure the aquarist that no sudden drop in temperature will occur in his tank.

A pH kit should be purchased for the salt-water aquarium. pH kits designed to accommodate the fresh-water range will not do for marine tanks. For salt water, a pH range from 7.7 to 8.4 should be encompassed by the color standard that accompanies the indicator in the set. A desirable reading ranges from 8.0 to 8.3. pH and its control will be discussed fully in Chapter 3.

Along with the equipment mentioned, the aquarist would do well to stock up on large-necked, five-gallon jugs. A collection of these will provide him with indispensable, safe storage containers. These jugs may be used on collecting trips and can serve as temporary hospital tanks.

Most hobbyists feel that the aquarium should be covered at all times. Either a Plexiglas or glass sheet can be used. Temporarily, Saran Wrap or vinyl plastic will serve the purpose.

We explained earlier that the lighting fixture should have glass between it and the aquarium water. If this glass has been fitted in the fixture, the sheet of plastic or glass need cover the aquarium only to the light. If, however, you have not fitted your light with an insert of glass, the glass will have to cover the top completely with your lighting fixture placed on top of it. In this case it is better to use glass, rather than Plexiglas. Plexiglas has a tendency to curl up if not anchored down in some way.

There are all types of equipment on the market these days for the hatching of brine shrimp, but the simple method of using a Pyrex baking dish with about a two-quart capacity is still very practical. The hatching of brine shrimp will be discussed in Chapter 4 in the section on feeding. Unless the aquarist wishes his fish room to be elaborately equipped, he can well afford to forego purchasing a brine-shrimp hatcher until the time he actually feels the need for one.

Ornaments and Decor

It is quite difficult for the novice to restrain himself from buying at least one piece each of all the delightful types of coral his dealer is apt to have on display. Coral is beautiful and has a decided place in the marine aquarium. It not only adds esthetically to the underwater seascape, but provides necessary hiding places for timid specimens and keeps mischievous ones busy guarding places they have appropriated for themselves. Also it is an aid in maintaining the alkalinity of the aquarium water.

It is well, however, to ascertain whether or not the coral you select has been chemically treated. Often bleaching and cleaning agents are used to whiten coral in order to make it even more attractive to the prospective customer. Unless the dealer is well informed, he will not realize that the chemically bleached coral can be indirectly deleterious to the well-being of the specimens in his customers' aquariums. Sun-bleached coral, of course, is quite safe in the aquarium but rather than take a chance as to how purchased coral has been whitened, it is better to purge it before placing it in the aquarium. This can be accomplished by placing the coral in an enamel pan. Cold water should then be added and the pan placed on a stove. The water should be allowed to come to a boil slowly. The boiling temperature ought to be retained for at least twenty minutes. After the coral is removed from the enamel pan, it should be placed in an oven at a low temperature for an hour. Soaking it afterward in aged fresh water is an added precaution. These treatments will leach out any chemicals that might have been used to whiten the coral.

Collected coral should be given a similar treatment but live coral never should be used in the aquarium. Pieces found high on the beach where they have been exposed to sun and rain for a long time are the only ones that should be used. This subject will be covered more thoroughly in Chapter 5.

What are commonly referred to as the organ-pipe corals should be avoided for although they are lovely to look at, they are tubular and their chambers provided places for bacteria to thrive and waste to collect. The staghorns, although they do not provide hiding places, are interesting in structure and safe enough to use. Large pieces of what is called dead coral rock are exceptionally fine, for not only are they found in interesting shapes, but they often contain cavities large enough for specimens to hide in. This type of coral is found high on the beaches of Florida, and because it looks like a kind of rock rather than coral, dealers seldom carry it. See Figures 17 and 60.

Coral that is safe to use in the aquarium must be hard to the core, that is, thoroughly dried out. Porous types should not be used. All pieces of coral should be treated as described previously in this chapter before it is placed in the aquarium.

Conch shells make fine aquarium pieces if the backs or spires have been cut away. Unless shells have been modified for aquarium use, there is a danger that they will become traps for waste materials or that tiny pieces of the animal that once inhabited them might still adhere to the inner walls. The decaying process of such pieces could very well pollute the aquarium water. Shells should be treated in the same manner recommended for coral, as they too are often bleached or polished for salability.

Sea fans and whips look extremely well outside the aquarium. They may be placed in back of it in such a way that they become part of a decorative backdrop and add much to the general beauty of the tank.

Again, we warn the aquarist to avoid any type of ornamentation made of metal, or questionable stones and rocks that may contain metal. Limestone is permissible, however, and can be used if coral is not available.

SUMMARY

All of the items we have mentioned for your shopping list are more or less essential for the maintenance of a salt-water aquarium. Many of these items are familiar to the fresh-water aquarist. As some pieces of fresh-water aquarium equipment, however, are not compatible with the salt-water hobby, we have gone over each item rather painstakingly at the risk of seeming dogmatic or becoming repetitious. The importance of these seemingly exaggerated exactitudes has been brought home to us many times through our own mistakes and those of others. Our extreme care is the result of long and at times painful experience.

Selection of Specimens and Pointers on Ordering Them

When you go over the interesting lists of fishes your dealer supplies, there are several factors to consider before ordering. The fishes you choose should, first of all, be small specimens. We know that there is nothing more beautiful than a French angel six inches from nose to tail, but your chances of keeping an inch-long specimen are much better. If your tank is a successful one, your fish will grow large before you know it.

If there is anything more beautiful than a French angel, it's two. But unless you've had an opportunity to study the specimens you are interested in before buying them, it's better to settle for one. Two French angels will usually battle it out until there is only one. This is not a hard and fast rule, for we have known and owned French angels who were friendly toward one another and have derived much pleasure from them. More often than not, however, two French angels spell trouble. Even two little fellows seldom make good tankmates. We stress this point here to illustrate the importance of knowing the characteristics and mannerisms of the various types of marine fishes before sending away for them or purchasing them from your dealer.

Read as much as you can about the fishes in which you are interested before you buy them. A thorough account of personality traits of the popular species of marine aquarium fishes will be given in this book and it would be a good idea to consider it before making your selections.

Do not buy too many specimens. Better to add them two at a time to your tank. Remember, too, that a fifteen-gallon tank will support only three or four small specimens comfortably.

Miscellaneous Specimens Offered by Dealers

One of the most fascinating aspects of the salt-water hobby is that it becomes to its devotees a constant adventure in discovery and learning. We mentioned before that only a sample of the countless colorful reef fishes adaptable to aquarium life have been presented to date.

Figure 5. THE HERMIT CRAB (*Clibanarius vittatus*)

This hermit crab has become very tame. It's peering out of its aquarium home at its owner in hopes that a tidbit might be offered. Note the marks in the sand behind it where it has dragged its shell.

The same is true of other kinds of living things that are cradled in the sea. Some of these creatures, however, have already become familiar to aquarists and frequently appear on dealers' lists. Like the various marine fishes, they, too, have definite personality traits of which the aquarist should be aware before adding them to his aquarium. Therefore, we are going over them rather carefully as they will be mentioned only in passing in later sections of this book.

The Hermit Crab (*Clibanarious vittatus*) Scavenger and Pet

The most successful scavenger for the marine aquarium is the hermit crab (*see* Figures 5 and 6), for this little fellow does a fine cleanup job. He contributes much in the way of keeping a salt-water tank healthy.

He moves about carrying his borrowed shell from corner to corner of the tank and there is little of the aquarium floor he doesn't cover in a day. Of course, he will eat the food the fishes miss, but make sure he gets his share because he really earns it. As he scuttles about, he leaves long trails in the sand, thereby loosening debris and waste material for the power filter to pick up. He will climb over coral and eat the algae that are growing there. He has been accused of attacking fishes but he is too slow and ponderous in his movements to harm a healthy fish. Aquarists who have seen him carry off a fish can be sure that the fish was dead before the crab reached it. Although the suit he wears under the shell he has appropriated for himself is drab in comparison to the gay colors his tankmates are wearing, he isn't without personality. If he outgrows his shell, have another larger one set aside for him. He will signify the bad fit of the old one by pacing up and down in a disturbing fashion.

If you look at him very carefully, you will notice he has two bright blue eyes mounted on stalks. These do not serve to locate his food; he depends rather on his sense of smell for this function. Even this is not too reliable a system in an aquarium, for often a hungry butterfly fish or angelfish will find a morsel before he does. He will go hungry if he

Robson Nelson

Figure 6.

A side view of the same hermit crab pictured in Figure 5.

doesn't have you looking out for his interests. When he learns you are his friend, he will take food from your fingers. If a scrap of food is left unmolested on the aquarium floor, he will eventually find it and at times he literally falls over backward in his enthusiasm to stake his claim.

You will become fond of this efficient little janitor and one or two small specimens are worthy of a home in your aquarium. Your shipper probably will have hermit crabs listed but if he doesn't, you might request one or two with your order. Ask for additional shells, too, so that you will not be caught short when your specimen has outgrown the one he was wearing when you first received him.

Plants

Some dealers or shippers may list plants, although transplanted salt-water grasses or algae seldom survive the operation. Most aquarists agree that ulva (sea lettuce), the most likely of the plants, usually curls up and dies before long and does more harm than good in that, unless taken out in time, it may cause the aquarium water to become foul. Although some skillful salt-water aquarists have been able to maintain ulva that they collected themselves, it is probably best for you to pass up any plants offered you.

On the other hand, if salt water is not at a premium for you as it is with aquarists living inland, you might very well experiment with plant life. Such experiments have been carried on by Craig Phillips, curator of the Seaquarium in Miami, Florida.[1]

Aquarists living inland who have a penchant for plant life may console themselves with the knowledge that if they are lucky enough to have a sunny place in the living room for their aquariums, they will have a substantial growth of algae on the walls of their tanks before long. It is understandable that this growth is not desirable on the front glass of the aquarium but when it appears on the ends and rear of the tank, it should not be removed. It is both beneficial to specimens as food and will serve to a degree as a water conditioner.

---

[1] Mr. Phillips gives a very fine report of such experiments in *The Aquarium,* May, 1956.

The Sea Anemone—Animal that looks like a flower

As you glance over the available specimens on your dealer's list you will, no doubt, find a reference to the sea anemones. These beautiful sea animals resemble flowers. Sometimes they are white with rose-tipped tentacles; often they are pink or lavender. Whatever color they may be, they are beautiful to look at and it is only natural for an aquarist to want several in his tank.

One sea anemone in a fifteen-gallon tank is almost more than enough as they cast off a slimy material, an accumulation of which is not desirable in the aquarium. They are hardy, however, and specimens have been kept for long periods of time in aquariums.

Sea anemones are animals and have to be fed. In their natural habitat, they stretch their graceful tentacles and catch their food in the currents of incoming and outgoing tides. They are thus able to keep well and healthy. In the aquarium, however, where food is not constantly available, the anemone should be hand fed. Tiny bits of shrimp (well rinsed under a running faucet) or beef should be dropped in the center of the flowerlike creature. The orifice in this section (*see* Figure 7) is actually the creature's mouth.

At times your anemone may lose its creamy whiteness. The brownish discoloration that may displease you is due to tiny brown algae that have for some reason become prevalent in your aquarium. As the anemone takes in water, the brown algae are absorbed and during the ingestive process the once-creamy white tentacles will now appear discolored. Such a change is quite normal and when the brown algae die down or are filtered out of the water, your anemone will become white again. In its natural environment the anemone is seldom seen unclouded in color. Unlike aquarium water, salt water in the sea is not filtered and depending on the kinds of crustacea and/or algae that are prevalent in it, the anemone you discover on the ocean floor will appear brownish-, pinkish-, or gray-white.

An anemone that is not doing well in an aquarium shrinks to an almost unrecognizable disc and remains this way until its owner removes it or it literally fades away. Upon occasion a healthy specimen will take on the attitude of a disc or a tube, but unless something is very wrong with it, it will blossom forth once more within a day or two.

Marine Studios, Marineland, Florida

Figure 7. THE SEA ANEMONE (*Condylactus passiflora*)

Note the orifice in the center of this flower-like marine animal. Food should be placed in the tentacles near this orifice which is the animal's mouth.

Anemones travel from place to place. Usually, you like your flowers to stay where you put them, and although you may be aware that your anemone is an animal, you are apt to regard it as a flower all the same. But don't become disgruntled because it has slowly edged off to a corner where you cannot see it to full advantage. You can move it by working a blade of a knife between it and the glass very gently. Since the anemone clings rather persistently to the spot it has chosen and seems to have a mind of its own, it will probably glide back to where it was the minute your back is turned. Better leave your flower alone and become a bit philosophical about its wanderlust. One of these days it will surprise you and show up exactly where you want it.

Enjoy the display of pink-tipped tentacles while you can—tomorrow it will be hidden behind a piece of coral in a spot that's most difficult for you to reach.

Incidentally, if in moving an anemone you forget to be as gentle as you should be and tear it, don't worry too much about it. It will heal eventually. A tear can be fatal, but the anemone's faculty of becoming whole again after an accident is often rather miraculous.

THE CORAL SHRIMP (*Stenopus hispidus*)—Wherever
he sits becomes a throne

The coral or banded shrimp is a lovely little fellow, coral-striped against white, and what he lacks in size, he makes up for in dignity (*see* Figure 8). When first acquired, he must be hand fed, but later he competes (with a regal air, of course) with the fishes for food by swimming up to the surface of the water. He has proved difficult to keep for any length of time in an aquarium but you might try him and be success-

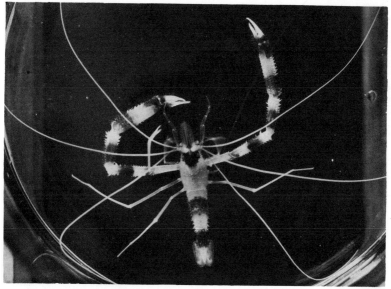

John H. Welsh

Figure 8. CORAL SHRIMP (*Stenopus hispidus*)

ful. More power to you! We think he might fare much better in natural sea water or a concentrate rather than in an artificial mix. Shells or coral should be included in the aquarium in which he is kept.

Specimens to Avoid in a Community Tank

Sea urchins, snails, slugs and starfish are all odd little fellows who are fascinating to most of us. Unless you maintain a tank for the unusual, however, excluding fishes entirely, they are best omitted. We have known aquarists who have kept urchins successfully in aquariums by themselves for long periods. Sea cucumbers should definitely be omitted; they let off a poison that is deadly to every other living member in the aquarium. We would be inclined to suggest that all such creatures be saved for a completely experimental tank rather than for the aquarium you plan as your showcase. Such a tank should be aerated and filtered as one set up for fishes would be. Algae should be encouraged for it seems to be a diet-supplement to almost all marine animals.

SUMMARY

After you have studied the personality traits of the specimens you wish to include in your aquarium, your next consideration will be your source. Your local dealer, if you have confidence in him as a marine aquarist, is, of course, your best choice. A careless dealer, or one un-schooled in the field, may offer you fishes that have been subjected to metal- or cement-poisoned water without realizing himself that his stock is earmarked for death. Now that shippers and retailers are becoming aware of the fact that marine tropicals require expert care, however, this danger is being eliminated.

Purchasing specimens from your local dealer relieves you of loss through poorly shipped stock. It also eliminates the necessity of picking up your specimens at the airport.

If your dealer does not carry marine specimens and it is necessary to have your fishes shipped by air, give the shipper specific instructions to wire you just before he puts the shipment on the plane. This message should contain information as to the flight number of the plane, the airline used and the expected time of arrival. Also, by now you should have learned the type of water the fishes will arrive in, that is, whether it will be natural salt water or a synthetic. If it is the latter, you should be informed as to the brand of salt-water mix your shipper is using. This information is necessary, as Neptune Salts, the artificial mix commonly used, should not be mixed with natural sea water.

You should be at the airport to receive the fishes when they come in for if they are left waiting in the cold, or in the hot sun, which-ever the case may be, they may be dead or in poor condition when you finally pick them up. Too much heat or cold can be fatal to them. If the shipment has been properly prepared, the plastic bag containing the specimens will have about two and a half gallons of water in it, and it will be partially blown up with oxygen. The plas-tic bag will be packed in a carton which is insulated with cardboard or newspaper. If it happens to be a cold time of the year, a special heating pad may be included in the carton.

Whether you have purchased your fishes from a local dealer or ordered them from a shipper, remember that if you don't exercise proper care in handling your marine pets yourself, all the expert at-tention they received before you owned them will be wasted, along with your investment.

Installing the Salt-Water Aquarium

Now that you have found the necessary equipment for your salt-water aquarium, perused your dealer's catalog, and armed yourself with all the available information on your hobby, it's time to set up your tank. You should do this several days before the arrival of your specimens as you will have many details to attend to then without having to cope with an unprepared aquarium.

Your first consideration will be the location in your living room or recreation room best suited for the tank. The ideal location is in a window with a southern exposure. During the summer months, light can be controlled with a shade or Venetian blind. Such a location is not always available so your second best choice is a space exposed to sun some part of the day only. Of course, you may have to depend completely on artificial light, which is all right but not nearly so desirable as sunlight.

If the aquarist has a choice of rooms, he will be wise to choose one where there is relatively little activity. Although salt-water fishes are not particularly shy, large groups of people, particularly those made up of a number of smokers, are to be avoided if possible. If entertaining is infrequent or confined to a few people at a time, there will be no danger in choosing the living room or recreation room for your tank.

When you have chosen your location, you can place your stand in the position most convenient for working, taking into consideration how it balances with the furniture of the room, and that there is an electric outlet nearby.

It might be a good idea at this time to have a conference with members of your family as to their opinion of the location you have chosen. You may receive some constructive ideas and avoid the chore of taking down your tank later because someone is sure that another corner of the room provides a better focal point than the one you have selected.

If you are using a Plexiglas or all-glass aquarium, be sure your stand has a solid top and not merely an iron frame.

The small amount of aquarium gravel or coral sand that you are going to use should be boiled and dried, ready to be sprinkled on the floor of the tank. Use just enough to cover the bottom of the aquarium. In no spot should it be more than a half-inch deep—a quarter of an inch is better. If you are using coarse coral sand or gravel, two or three handfuls of fine beach sand (boiled and dried) should be added.

Arrange your coral according to your esthetic values but remember that it is functional as well as decorative. Some little reef fish is going to claim it and guard it with its life, so place it where the holes are most accessible. Put another piece far enough away from it so that this same little reef character won't try to guard both of them. Every piece or head of coral you use in your tank will become some small creature's castle, so allow considerable space between each piece.

By this time you have familiarized yourself with the various types of synthetic salt mixes available on the market as well as the salt-water concentrates, and you have decided which one you are going to use. In any case, now that it is time to have water in your tank, you should have a supply of aged or distilled water on hand, unless, of course, you are planning to use natural salt water. If you have a supply of the latter, it should be filtered and stored in a dark place until you are ready for it. (Synthetic mixes and salt-water concentrates are discussed in Chapter 3, as well as the maintenance of salt water in the aquarium.)

Follow the manufacturer's directions to the letter. They will appear on the package of the salt-water mix you have selected. The manufacturer has tried and tested his formula and the results he has obtained are the basis for his instructions. If you have chosen a salt-water concentrate, the directions on its container should be carefully followed.

After you have poured water into your tank, set up your filtration system. Turn it on after your salt-water mix has dissolved. Your filtering material (glass wool or nylon pad) should be employed now regardless of the kind of water you are using. Keep your water aerated during the period you are waiting for your fishes and don't forget to have a healthy batch of brine-shrimp eggs hatching the day your fishes arrive. Your thermostatically controlled heater should be operating in order to avoid adjusting the temperature of the tank water any more than you have to when the specimens arrive.

Introducing Specimens to Their New Home

The day your fishes arrive it might be a good idea to have the following articles in the room you have chosen for your aquarium:

> Thermometer (aquarium type)
> Enameled pail or pan (gallon capacity)
> Extra air line in working condition
> Hydrometer
> Small hand net

All of these items must be scrupulously clean and free from soap film or any other substance. Also, your hands should be scrubbed. A tiny bit of tobacco caught under a fingernail could be the undoing of all your efforts.

Before you attempt to remove your specimens from the container they have arrived in, check both temperature and salinity of the water your fishes have been shipped in or have been living in while they were in your dealer's possession.

If the temperature in your aquarium is cooler than that of the water the fishes are in, you may bring it up by heating a portion of it in an enameled pail or pan. Be sure that there are no cracks or places where the enamel has been chipped in the pan you use. Stand near the water as you heat it and do not allow it to become more than warm. When it is warm to the touch, pour it into your tank. Check again and if the temperature in both the container with fishes in it and the tank water are the same, you are ready to read the salinity of both waters. However, if you find the aquarium water is still too cool, you will have to repeat the heating process. While you are working, you should have air running into the shipping container so that your specimens are comfortable while waiting to be placed in their new home. Sometimes the process of adjusting temperatures and salinities takes longer than you might guess. If, on the other hand, the water in the container is cooler, than that in the aquarium, you might put a heater into it. As it holds only a small amount of water, it will not take long to raise the temperature a few degrees. It is a mistake to move fishes from warm to cold water and it is better not to move them from cold to warm water when the difference is more than three degrees. In the case of fishes that have suffered a great drop in temperature while in transit, however, do not wait to bring the temperature up in their container, but get them into warm water as soon as possible.

When the temperatures are adjusted to your satisfaction, you may test the salinity of both the container water and the aquarium water. A difference of two points is not enough to worry about. However, should the reading in your tank be considerably lower than that of the water in which your fishes are waiting, you can bring it up by adding a good grade of aquarium salt if you are using natural sea water; or more of the salt mix or concentrate, whichever you are using.

Always test the temperature before reading salinity as the temperature of the water affects the salinity reading. If the water is the same temperature, this ceases to be a factor.

The normal salinity reading of water collected from the Florida Keys is 1.025. If the water your dealer or shipper has been using reads higher than this, add some distilled or aged tap water to the container. Do this cautiously as you do not want to add too much; a rapidly decreased salinity may cause the specimens discomfort.

When the salinity of the water in the container and aquarium has been adjusted, you are ready to place your salt-water fishes in their new home. It is better to catch them in a clean bowl or dish than with a hand net. If your dealer has used the type of salts that cannot be mixed with natural sea water or other types of synthetic mixes (Neptune Salts) and you are not going to use this particular brand, you will have to transfer your specimens with a hand net. In either case, use care and economy of motion. Get the fishes into their new home as quickly and gently as possible.

If a fish is dropped in transfer, never pick it up with a dry hand or cloth. Wet your hand or a clean cloth quickly and pick the specimen up firmly but gently. Get it back into water as soon as possible. Gently urge the fish to move with a plastic wand or hand net if it sinks to the bottom and lies quietly. Fishes that are transferred at night also sometimes act in this manner and should be urged to move.

Fishes that have been in transit too long for the amount of oxygen available to them, come to the surface of the water and blow and gasp. If they have been in this condition for a long period, they often die. However, if your fishes arrive in this condition get an air line to them as fast as possible. A good strong flow of air should be passed into the water.

It is not advisable to add a newly acquired fish to an established aquarium containing well-adjusted specimens. The newcomer should be placed in a five- or ten-gallon auxiliary tank, or even a five-gallon glass jug can be used for the purpose. Here it can be observed for disease for the next ten to fourteen days. In this instance the water in which the fish has arrived should be made to comply with the water in the observation tank. Whatever correction is made, however, make sure that it is not drastic. Salt-water fishes are extremely sensitive and although a change may not be fatal, it will weaken their resistance. Any kind of change should be made gradually, with the exception of fishes that have been chilled in transit.

The auxiliary tank should be well aerated and a piece of coral supplied for the specimen's comfort. During the observation period, the water in the auxiliary tank or jug can be gradually made to comply with that in the aquarium proper. If in this period the fish shows signs of disease or abnormal behavior, we suggest you refer to Chapter 4 where this subject is covered.

These precautionary measures not only give the new specimen a resting and adjusting period but may save all your well-established fishes from contracting an infection.

If your fishes have been on a plane for several hours and seem frightened and upset upon arrival, it may be a good idea to wait an hour after they have been placed in their new home before feeding them. Even then, feed them lightly as they may not accept food at once. Should they appear to adjust to their new environment immediately, you may feed them right away. A light sprinkling of brine shrimp should be eagerly accepted, or some minutely shredded raw beef or rinsed raw shredded shrimp. Lettuce should be included with the first meal; in the absence of algae, it is very important to establish this vegetable as part of the regular diet. The lettuce should be in tiny pieces, approximately the size of a pinhead. In any case, hand-feed your specimens and be sure the food is being eaten before offering any more. Chapter 4 will cover the feeding of fishes more thoroughly.

Marine Aquarium Management

We have covered a great deal of ground in this chapter and have purposely skipped over the principles behind many of the rules we have set down in order to stay with the subject at hand. Further on, you will discover the basis for each suggestion and learn why each is important and how much latitude you have for modifications.

If your tank has been set up properly, with equipment that is chemically stable in salt water, many of your troubles are over and maintenance is rather simple. Nevertheless, problems do have a tendency of showing up at the most inopportune times, so we shall anticipate some of them and try to help you meet them in the best way we know.

Cleanliness is probably the first prophylactic measure. If your filtering system does not pick up waste products, you will need a long, glass dip-tube for this chore.

Suspended material in the water should be kept at a minimum by filtration. The power filter performs this particular chore superbly well. If you are using standard filtration, the suspended material will eventually be cleared away if you are careful to wash out the filtering material each time it becomes permeated with algae.

If your hermit crab has not cleaned up the excess food you have given your fishes, take this surplus out with your dip-tube. Never allow it to remain in the tank overnight.

It is never wise to use what fish pathologists term "shot-gun therapy," that is, the administering of drugs indiscriminately in the aquarium proper. In some instances, you may treat the tank by adding certain medications to the aquarium water but only when you have a definite goal in mind. An injured fish or one that is ailing from an unknown cause should always be removed from the tank to the hospital aquarium for individual treatment. Methods of treatment will be given in Chapter 4. We mention treatments now merely to point out that applying one drug after another to the aquarium is playing with trouble; eventually you will find it necessary to make a complete change of water. If you must experiment with a drug, do so in a small hospital tank. It is far easier to replace a few gallons of water than twenty-five or fifty.

Do not leave your tank lights on all night. Your specimens need a period of darkness. If you see your fishes change color slightly during the evening, or if they tend to stay in their nighttime places, put their tank lights out, for they obviously want to sleep.

If you have been out after dark or if your aquarium is in a room that has become dark because of the hour, do not suddenly turn on the tank lights. If you want to do so later, you may, but put on the room lights first and when your fishes have adjusted to that light, you can put their lights on. Sudden light causes some fishes to jump out of the tank if it isn't well covered. Even when a cover is in use, they may strike it as they jump and become bruised and injured.

Do not permit drastic changes of temperature to occur in your aquarium. Unless your thermostatically controlled heater is worn out or imperfect, this should not happen. Aquariums that are kept in rooms subject to temperature changes should be equipped with thermostatically controlled heaters. Somewhere between 75 and 80 degrees

Fahrenheit might be considered ideal. In summer, of course, higher temperatures sometimes prevail. During such warm periods, the aquarist should keep the shades down in the room and try to maintain it as cool as possible. Only when the aquarium water reads over 90 degrees Fahrenheit is it necessary to float clean, sealed, glass jars containing ice cubes in the aquarium. In such an emergency, the aquarium can be covered with Saran wrap. This is necessary because the fishes may become alarmed and frightened by the strange floating objects and try to jump out of the tank.

*p*H and salinity readings should be kept constant. Both these topics will be discussed in Chapter 3.

Sunlight is beneficial to the marine tank. However, if you live in the tropics, or in a place where the temperature zooms up to 100° Fahrenheit during the hottest part of the day, close the Venetian blind or pull down the shade during this period. Temperatures in the nineties are harmful to your pets. Readings from 70 to 74° are good ones and it will be well to try to maintain them constantly if possible.

When you are showing your pets to a friend and one fish is under the coral or busy in a corner where he cannot be seen easily, don't rap on the tank to frighten him out of his corner. Better to offer him a feeding of brine shrimp or wait until he comes forward of his own will to be introduced. Actually, one of the outstanding personality traits of marine fishes is their friendliness. Usually, all the aquarist has to do is appear before his tank, and his pets crowd to the front to greet him and try to beguile him into giving them a handout. When they don't perform in this fashion it is a signal to the conscientious aquarist that something is wrong. If, however, the fishes have never adjusted because they have been subjected to rappings and other types of rough treatment, they have become oversensitive to movement and sounds. Some adults and children have good aquarium manners instinctively; others have to be reminded to watch theirs.

Whenever it becomes necessary to put your hands into the aquarium water, wash them carefully and rinse them well, making sure you get all the soap off in the process. Hand lotion or perfume on the hands can be deleterious and minute pieces of tobacco caught under the fingernails can be fatal.

Feed carefully. A feeding of brine shrimp in the morning and shredded, washed raw shrimp or raw beef in the evening, augmented by the smallest bits of lettuce you can produce is a happy feeding routine. If you or someone who is an experienced aquarist is home during the day, more frequent feedings might be advantageous. Your specimens are very young and small feedings at frequent intervals is a good plan if you are able to manage it.

If you begin to notice that your fishes have changed their pace of activity, or that their fins are folded and pinched, you should recognize at once that something you have done has caused this unhappy circumstance. If they begin to die, do not rush out and purchase more fishes before you have considered every step you have taken to discover the cause of the upset in your tank. Has your water been exposed to metal? Have you added a medication to the aquarium on the advice of an interested but uninformed friend? Have you overfed and allowed the excess food to collect on the floor of your tank? Have you used questionable coral or other types of ornamentation that might cause chemical changes in the water? Have you introduced a new specimen without isolating it for the suggested length of time?

If you have done any of these things, or a combination of them, you need a change of water more than you need new fishes. A fresh stock would only meet with the same fate as did your first collection of specimens.

Refer to the chapter on disease in this book (Chapter 4) and try to discover where you have gone wrong. If the trouble is toxicity and you catch it soon enough, you might be able to save your specimens. If the trouble is pathological, you may still be able to save them.

After you have considered all the factors carefully and cannot discover where you erred in the management of your tank and you have had your fishes for less than a month, you might consider their source. If you have had them over a month, however, and they seemed perfectly happy at first, the chances are that you have overlooked some damaging factor in your own maintenance of the aquarium.

In any case, it is a good idea to start treatment with new water, unless after reading Chapter 4 you decide the trouble is pathological. If toxicity is suspected, change the fishes into new water and new quarters, even if it means putting them in five-gallon aerated jars. Take down your aquarium and discard the water, and then, of course, remove the cause of the toxicity. If you suspect the cement used in the construction of your aquarium, you cannot use it again for salt-water specimens. A Plexiglas tank might be substituted, or a tank that is constructed especially for salt-water use.

Whatever the trouble is, you may be sure that either you or the dealer from whom you purchased your specimens did something wrong. Marine-tank management is as precise as arithmetic. Failure is ninety-nine per cent due to error in judgment. Probably the remaining one per cent is, too. There isn't a chance element in it except in the source of the fishes. Although disease is frequently suspected as being the cause of ailing fishes, very often it is not. In our experience the most common cause for failure has been toxicity. This is, of course, the reason we have stressed so frequently the types of materials and equipment that are safe to use in salt water. If your equipment has been thoughtfully selected and its compatibility with the salt-water hobby considered, most of your troubles are behind you.

In the past, when we were not so aware of the need for materials impervious to the onslaught of salt water, we would send fishes that had died from causes we were unable to determine to fish pathologists for examination, certain that the report would come back indicating that some salt-water parasite was present. Even when disease or bacteria were present on the fish, we were told that the cause of death was more likely to be toxic conditions existing in the aquarium. Shortly after fishes die, the bacteria count rises rapidly, making an accurate determination as to the cause of death impossible. One by one, we eliminated questionable materials from our experiments, and finally, when we turned to Plexiglas tanks, our worries, insofar as toxicity was concerned, were over.

The maintenance of marine aquariums is a precise science with little margin for error. It is to be recommended for the advanced aquarist or the hobbyist willing to follow directions as closely as he would if he were an amateur photographer, chef, or gardener.

When proper conditions exist in the salt-water aquarium, marine fishes are hardy and have long life spans in comparison to many fresh-water fishes. We sincerely promise the serious aquarist that his success in the salt-water hobby will be both stimulating and satisfying.

CHAPTER 3

Salt Water for the Aquarium

*Maintenance of Salt Water in the Aquarium ·
pH Control · Salinity Control · Natural Sea
Water vs. Synthetic Salt Water and the Salt-
Water Concentrates · Light and the Marine
Aquarium · Detection of Toxic Conditions in
Marine Aquarium Water · Collecting Natural
Sea Water.*

Maintenance of Salt Water in the Aquarium

Scientific papers containing information particularly useful to the
aquarist on the subject of "captured" sea water are few in number. Although sea water has been studied from many points of view, the
aquarist's interest in it has been almost completely neglected. In a
way, this is an asset, for few conflicting opinions exist in the papers that
have been presented on salt water containing marine animals in
closed-system or circulating aquariums. In one paper reporting the
chemical changes that occur in "captured" sea water, we learn that
the medium can be kept in condition normal enough to sustain fishes
without too much difficulty. Herein lies the key to successful marine
aquarium management, for without such promise, the maintenance
of salt-water fishes in a closed-system aquarium would be impossible.

In addition to the fact that sea water contains almost every known
chemical element in quantities that vary from one time or place to another, that it is far more concentrated with minute life than is fresh
water, and that few materials remain chemically stable when in contact with it, countless unusual facts have been discovered regarding it

59

by scientists who have made it a subject for lifetime study. As the aquarist, however, is chiefly concerned with it as a medium in which he can keep marine specimens in a healthy condition, we shall limit our remarks to that phase of the subject. We have stressed in Chapter 2 the need for equipment that will obviate the danger of deleterious chemical change in aquarium water.

The minute life in "captured" sea water cannot be supported in the aquarium as it would be in the ocean. Therefore, it is most advisable to remove as much of it as possible from freshly collected sea water before using it in the tank. This can be partially accomplished by filtration. The water can be poured through nylon filtering material or some other type of inert filtering agent such as quartz or glass wool. The living matter in sea water is made up of protozoa (one-celled minute animals), phytoplankton (minute plant organisms) and bacteria. Although filtering removes a large proportion of this material, the sea water will still contain more minute life than is desirable. So, after the filtering process, the water should be stored in glass jugs in complete darkness for a period of about three weeks. The bulk of the living matter it contains will perish during this period, for without light the minute plant life will die off, thereby starving the tiny animals which feed on it. This water should be filtered once more before it is put in the aquarium so that the organic material, the remains of the minute life, can be eliminated. Of course, not all of the living organisms have been removed from the water, but the over-all count has been reduced to a point where the aquarist can proceed with reasonable assurance.

As soon as this water is exposed to light, minute plants will again begin to thrive. No matter how scrupulously clean the aquarium is kept, or how carefully the rules of good housekeeping have been observed, tiny living things, including bacteria, will continue to exist in the aquarium. The object is to keep the count as low as possible. If any kind of biological balance is to be met, let it begin from there.

All forms of life in the aquarium from the lowest forms of bacteria to the fishes themselves respire, and wherever respiration occurs, carbon dioxide is produced and carbohydrates and oxygen are absorbed. On the other hand, although the algae in an aquarium give off waste products due to respiration, they also contain a pigment called chlorophyll, the essential catylist in the process known as photosynthesis. Algae then are capable of photosynthetic action and produce carbohydrates and oxygen in the presence of light. During this process they utilize waste products and carbon dioxide as raw materials. To say that appreciable amounts of solvent waste are consumed as nutrients by the growing algae would be promising too much, but they do dispense with some of it and also serve as food for the fishes.

In a paper by P. F. Stowell, it is stated that a glass jar, placed in full sunlight, was filled with sea water with only algae and bacteria present. In time the carbon dioxide was utilized to a point that the pH climbed to a reading over 9 which, of course, is highly alkaline. In aquariums where specimens along with algae and bacteria are present, such a reading would never occur. In the latter case a kind of balance is achieved, the carbon dioxide and waste materials acting as a brake against high alkalinity readings and the algae serving, along with buffers in the water, as a check against high acidity readings. This is not a true balance, of course, for without the measures of good housekeeping, filtration and aeration, the desirable conditions could not be sustained for any length of time.

The aeration system and methods of filtration are for the most part mechanical and to say that these measures are necessary is almost sufficient. Good housekeeping, however, is a broad term that necessitates a finite explanation.

Feeding methods relate to good or bad housekeeping. Overfeeding must be carefully avoided in marine aquariums. Although hermit crabs will eventually reach uneaten food, they should not be depended upon for this chore. For even before they reach a bit of shredded raw shrimp or beef, decomposition will have begun. It is far better to hand-feed specimens when beef, raw shrimp or lettuce is being offered. If you cannot take time for such a feeding, brine shrimp should be provided; postpone the raw shrimp or beef feeding to another hour when you have more time.

All insolvent waste and dying vegetation should be removed from the aquarium. If the filtering system does not pick up such material, it should be siphoned off or removed with a dip tube. Bits of decomposing vegetation and excrement on the aquarium floor create a perfect breeding medium for bacteria. A cushion of deep sand only worsens the situation.

A revolving water system should be established. This involves removal of a portion of the aquarium water about once every six weeks. This water should be carefully filtered and placed in dark storage, where it should remain for at least three weeks. Water that has been resting from the previous change should be filtered and poured into the aquarium. In this way, the aquarist will always have some water in dark storage (in whatever quantity he may deem desirable). Water can be used over and over again when this method is employed and whether artificial salt water, concentrate, or natural sea water is used, a system of this type should be followed.

Dark storage provides a partial elimination of minute life and a reduction of certain waste products that result from respiration. Stowell points out that sea water that has been filtered and stored in the manner we have described shows an increase of nitrate, phosphate, and silicates, but that these changes are not drastic enough to be injurious to specimens. The reduction of ammonia and bacterial content, on the other hand, is highly beneficial.

An aquarist may test one of the benefits gained from dark storage by examining, under an inexpensive microscope, samples of freshly collected sea water, water taken directly from the aquarium, and water just out of dark storage. He will find considerable signs of life in both the freshly collected sea water and water removed from the aquarium. However, the water just out of dark storage will show little or no sign of small living things.

This test will show about the same results regardless of whether natural or artificial salt water is used. We have found that artificial salt water which has been used in an aquarium over a period of time is as active with minute life as natural sea water.

To summarize briefly, we might say that aeration, filtration and good housekeeping are important factors in keeping salt water in a condition acceptable to the highly fastidious reef fishes. A system employing dark storage will do much to eliminate high bacterial counts and to remove solvent waste products which cannot be otherwise reduced. This system will also serve as an economy measure since it will eliminate a continual need for newly collected or newly mixed water.

We should like to point out as a word of caution that water that is suspected of being toxic should be discarded immediately. Recovery of such contaminated sea water should never be attempted.

*p*H Control

The aquarist applies the term *p*H when he is expressing the degree of acidity or alkalinity of the water in his tank. The term literally means *potential hydrogen ion.* A *p*H scale was devised in 1909 which serves as a measure for acidity or alkalinity existing in solution (*see* Figure 9).

The zero mark on the *p*H scale indicates the strongest degree of acidity and 14 expresses the highest degree of alkalinity. A reading of 7.0 represents a neutral reading where neither a condition of acidity nor alkalinity exists. Actually a balance of the hydrogen ions $(H+)$ and hydroxyl ions $(OH-)$ has been established. Any reading below 7 would indicate a condition of acidity, progressing in strength from 6.9 down to 0. Any reading from 7.1 to 14 would indicate alkalinity, progressing in strength from 7.1 up to 14. A reading of *p*H 1 is one tenth as strong as 0 in acidity. A reading of *p*H 2 would be only one hundredth as strong as 0 in acidity. Each point on the scale is ten times as strong or weak as the next point to it. Reading zero, the strongest point of acidity, and moving up the scale to 7, we have reached the balance between acidity and alkalinity. Leaving 7.0, we move into the alkaline side of the scale, increasing in strength until the peak of alkalinity, a reading of 14, is reached.

A *p*H reading of vinegar, for instance, would be approximately 2.3. Apples would give a reading of about 3, whereas sea water, the medium in which we are particularly interested, might give us a reading from 8.2 to 8.4, depending upon the time of year the water was collected.

| 0 | 1 | 2 | 3 | 4 | 5 | 6 | 7 | 8 | 9 | 10 | 11 | 12 | 13 | 14 |

ACID   ALKALINE

Figure 9. *p*H SCALE

In the fresh-water hobby particular pH readings are often suggested for certain fishes. For example, if an aquarist were interested in breeding neon tetras, he would strive for a pH condition of 6.5, which is on the acid side. However, variances in pH are not recommended in the salt-water hobby, although a margin of difference can be allowed. Readings within the range of 8.0 to 8.3 are safe for specimens, although an effort should be made to establish and maintain one point in that field.

There are many systems of measuring pH. They fall into two groups. One is called the electrometric method, which entails the use of a pH meter. This is a highly sensitive instrument but as most aquarists do not have access to such equipment, we shall go on to the other group which covers the colorimetric methods. These employ dyes which, when added to samples of water, change in color, depending upon the acid or alkaline condition, or pH, of the samples being tested. Kits are available that usually consist of a small bottle of dye (or indicator) and a color chart. Each color on the chart is captioned with the degree of pH it represents. A sample of water which has had a few drops of the indicator added to it will change in color. The color that matches it on the chart will give the approximate pH of the sample. Another type of test kit consists of a roll of chemically treated paper. When a piece of this paper is dipped in a sample of the water to be tested, its color changes and the color that comes closest to matching it on the chart reveals the approximate pH of the sample.

These kits cover different ranges on the pH scale. The marine aquarist must select a kit that includes in its range the readings of 8.0 to 8.3. The dye used in such a kit is often phenol red. A small bottle of this indicator can be used without a color chart if the aquarist does not have one. A sample of freshly collected sea water should be tested and the shade of pink resulting from the test can be used as a guide. A stoppered test tube containing this should be saved for a standard, although after a considerable passage of time the color may change. The sample can also be matched with a piece of paper, as close to the shade of pink as possible for use in future readings.

Although phenol red is usually mentioned as the indicator for salt-water pH testing, we believe a dye with a wider range is more desirable. The range of phenol red is from 6.8 to 8.4, the color change running from yellow (6.8) to red (8.4). Certainly the 6.8 point on the acid side is adequate, but the 8.4 limits the aquarist to an alkalinity that barely leaves the safety zone. Cresol red is worth considering, as it includes 7.2 to 8.8 in its range, running from yellow to red.

Keeping the desirable pH range from 8.0 to 8.3 in mind, we shall now consider the causes for change in pH.

A tank where circulation, filtration, and aeration are constant will not show much change in pH unless it gets little sunlight or is overcrowded. Stowell reports that water stored in a glass container in the sunlight, without specimens present, climbed to a pH of 9. Water stored in the dark in a glass container tended to go slightly acid. These findings suggest that tanks placed in direct sunshine during the summer months should be shaded to some extent even though the presence of specimens will retard any tendency toward extreme alkalinity (8.4 or over). Aquarists who, on the other hand, keep their tanks in artificial light, or subdued light should watch the pH of their water rather carefully, for under such lighting conditions an acid condition may very well develop.

Too little aeration is a cause of acidity. A reliable test to check the aeration system is to place a sample of aquarium water in a small test tube and add a pinch of slaked lime. If the water remains clear as the lime sinks to the bottom, there is little free carbon dioxide in the water which means that the aquarium is being aerated well enough. If on the other hand, the water becomes milky, the aquarium water is not receiving adequate aeration and the system will have to be changed in some way. This condition will not exist if a power filter is used; stepping up the amount of air going into the tank will help. Of course, if the tank is hopelessly overcrowded, no aerating system will correct the condition. Another tank is in order, or some of the specimens should be given to aquarist friends. Although the aquarist may not wish to give up the fishes, he will be obliged to do so in order to save them.

Acidity is also caused by an accumulation of food and waste products. Good housekeeping has been stressed previously but here again its importance is evident.

If an acid condition is discovered, the following steps should be taken. A portion of the aquarium water should be removed and filtered and placed in dark storage. Either fresh water or water that has been in dark storage should replace it. By fresh water we mean either newly mixed artificial salt water, recently collected sea water, or diluted concentrate, whichever of these the aquarist has been using. The aeration system should be stepped up or the power filter should be allowed to run for over an hour at a time. Be sure the newly added water has been checked for temperature and density. If corrections were found necessary, they should have been made before the water was added to the aquarium. The stored water will be slightly on the acid side as we have explained before, but aeration will correct this condition.

If the pH reading still shows acid after these measures have been taken, sodium bicarbonate will have to be added to the aquarium water. The waste products in the water have accumulated to the point that the natural bicarbonates in the water have been displaced. Because the degree of sodium bicarbonate needed to correct the aquarium can vary greatly, it is suggested that the aquarist feel his way in adding the corrective medium. A quarter of a teaspoon of sodium bicarbonate should be added to a small portion of the aquarium water that has been removed for this purpose. When this is mixed, pour it back into the aquarium through the filter chamber. The air should be stepped up or the power filter turned on. After an hour or so, the aquarist should again take a reading. If his aquarium water still reads on the acid side, the above process should be repeated with the same amount of sodium bicarbonate. It is far better to proceed cautiously than to use a large quantity of bicarbonate all at once. This gradual procedure is a safeguard against using too much sodium bicarbonate and will also save the fishes from an unnecessarily sharp change in pH.

The use of sodium bicarbonate is a last resort to correct a condition which cannot otherwise be adjusted. If the rules of salt-water aquarium management are followed carefully, such correction will be unnecessary. Many tanks that have been in operation for over a year have not required such treatment, because their owners have followed the rules of good aquarium management.

To summarize briefly, we might list some additional causes we have not touched on which might create an acid condition in the aquarium:

1. Large hermit crabs in tanks of a fifteen-gallon capacity or less.
2. Large specimens (large angels for instance) in tanks of a fifteen-gallon capacity or less.
3. High density (or salinity), which steps up the metabolism of specimens, in overcrowded tanks.
4. Great quantities of live brine shrimp which have not been consumed by the fishes.

The following tend to keep the aquarium water on the alkaline side:

1. Tanks that are in full sunlight with algae growing on sides and rear walls.
2. The presence of coral.
3. The presence of a thin layer of sand composed of crushed shells and coral, such as is found along the Florida coast.

Suggested Reading

C. M. Breder, Jr., and T. H. Howley, "The Chemical Control of Closed Circulating Systems of Sea Water in Aquaria for Tropical Marine Fishes," *Zoologica,* New York Zoological Society, January 28, 1931.

H. W. Harvey, *The Chemistry and Biology of Sea Water,* Cambridge, 1945.

Salinity Control

Sea water is heavier than fresh water because it contains more dissolved matter. There is about a quarter of a pound of dissolved material to a gallon of sea water. Water lost through evaporation causes the water in the aquarium to become heavier, or to possess a greater salinity.

Because fishes are sensitive to changes of salinity, when an appreciable amount of water is lost through evaporation it is necessary for the aquarist to add distilled or aged tap water to the aquarium. Fresh water is added because it is fresh water that is lost and not dissolved matter.

The aquarist can check the aquarium now and then to keep posted on how much water is lost, or what the density of the water is by using a small instrument called a hydrometer (*see* Figure 10). This is a sealed glass tube that is weighted at the bottom so that when it is placed in water it assumes a vertical position. The part of the tube that is in the

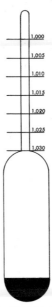

Figure 10. HYDROMETER

water is an elongated bulb and the upper end is usually a thin straight tube which is calibrated. Where the water line comes on the calibrated tube tells the aquarist what the density or salinity of the water is.

Because the weight of the water varies with its temperature, the hydrometer is calculated for a given temperature. Usually hydrometers are calculated for 60° Fahrenheit. Cold water is heavier than warm water so that water at about 40°, when read with a hydrometer, seemingly would have a higher salinity than when the same water was read at a temperature of 60°. Aquarium water is, however, kept at a temperature of approximately 72° Fahrenheit. In order to get an accurate salinity reading, the aquarist should remove about a quart of the aquarium water and bring its temperature down to 60°, the temperature for which his hydrometer is calibrated. He should then take a reading. If the reading at 60° is the one he wants, he knows that the salinity of the water in his aquarium is correct. He should now read the aquarium water. This reading is the one he will want to maintain, so he should make a note of it for future testing. This reading is the adjusted one, reflecting the change of hydrometric reading due to temperature difference. A rule for such adjustment is approximately as follows: a 12° drop in temperature equals about a two-point increase in salinity reading, that is, water at 72° might read 1.023 on the hydrometer. If the same water is chilled to 60°, the hydrometer reading will be approximately 1.025.

The point of salinity at which the aquarist keeps his aquarium water is often modified by his experience and opinion. Water collected off the Florida Keys shows a reading of 1.025. This, then, is the normal salinity for Florida marine tropicals. If the salinity increases, the metabolism of the specimens becomes more active. This means that in water of high salinity (1.030, for example) the fishes eat more, give off more waste material and usually become more active. Dealers often keep their fishes in a high salinity because specimens, becoming more active, give the appearance of being in particularly good health. It is our opinion, however, that the salinity should be brought down gradually to a point of 1.022. This decreased salinity tends to slow the fishes down. They eat less, of course, and give off less waste materials. Quarreling is less, too, and although they are active, they seem to do better in the closed-system aquarium when the salinity is brought down somewhat.

When a shipment of fishes arrives, it is not wise to change the density or salinity abruptly from, for example, 1.030 to 1.022. Such a change will cause the specimens great distress and they might go into what is called osmotic shock. The water the fishes arrive in should be checked for both temperature and density. New specimens, of course, are never introduced into the established aquarium upon arrival. The water in the aquarium or five-gallon glass jug which is to serve as an isolation ward should be made to correspond with the water the fishes arrive in. One or two points lower in salinity will not do any harm. If the water the fishes arrive in reads 1.030, the water in the isolation ward should be brought up to at least 1.028. Temperatures should be the same but if the isolation tank shows a slightly higher temperature, no adjustment is necessary. If the water the specimens have been shipped in is chilled, the newcomers can be put in the isolation aquarium immediately if the salinity reads the same or is two points lower (or higher). On the other hand, should the water in the isolation tank be colder, heating will be necessary.

Salinity, or density, may be raised by adding any type of aquarium salt; if artificial salts are being used, more of the brand that has been selected should be added to the water.

New specimens should be kept in the isolation ward from ten to fourteen days. During this period, the salinity of the water can be adjusted gradually to that of the water in the aquarium which is to be their permanent home. The isolation ward should be well-aerated and the fishes should be made as comfortable as possible in their temporary quarters. If there are more than three small specimens, a larger isolation ward than a five-gallon jug will be necessary. Another five-gallon jug, of course, can be used.

Thus the isolation ward serves as a conditioning tank where specimens can be slowly adjusted to the salinity and temperature readings that will prevail in their permanent home. It serves many other purposes, also, which will be discussed in later chapters.

The salinity of the aquarium proper should be checked at least every two weeks. A simple way to determine how much water has been lost through evaporation is to use a small piece of Scotch tape as a marker by sticking it on the outside of the aquarium at the desired water level. When the water level is appreciably below the marker (over an inch), distilled or aged tap water should be used to raise it. The hydrometer should be used occasionally even if this system is used.

The use of distilled water to replace water that has been lost through evaporation is a safeguard against an accumulation of additional dissolved salts that may be present in tap or well water. We have used aged tap water without any apparent ill-effects, as have many marine aquarists. Unless the hobbyist lives miles away from cities and other highly industrial areas, rainwater is not desirable for aquarium use.

Natural Sea Water vs. Synthetic Salt Water and Salt-Water Concentrates

Synthetic salt water formulas are not something new under the sun. There is a paper included in Volume 9 of the *Bulletin* of the United States Fish Commission, dated October 1, 1884, by H. E. Hoffman, entitled *Artificial Sea Water for the Aquaria.* In it, Mr. Hoffman relates rather charmingly that the Berlin Aquarium suffered from an ailment which the Berliners, who were inordinately proud of their public aquarium, referred to as "sea-sickness," or an insufficient supply of fresh sea water. The use of artificial salt water seemed to be the answer to the problem. Mr. Hoffman goes on to say that after many failures in compounding a formula that would successfully support sea animals, one was discovered which proved satisfactory. He lists the ingredients as being approximately as follows:

> 13¼ gallons of pure well water
> 46½ ounces common salt
> 3½ ounces sulfate of magnesium
> 5¼ ounces chlorate of magnesium
> 2   ounces sulfate of potassium

His directions advise that the purest chemicals must be used and each ingredient must be dissolved in part of the water by itself; then they may be mixed together and allowed to stand quietly for a few hours so that impurities may settle to the bottom. All floating particles should be removed and the mixture should be poured into another vessel. Fresh water, preferably hard well water, is added until the hydrometer gives the desired reading. This will produce about thirteen and a quarter gallons of sea water, Mr. Hoffman tells us, and goes on to say that this mixture also contains small quantities of soda, iron, and potash. He is not too clear as to how these latter ingredients are added but he probably assumes that they occur in the hard water. He suggests that newly manufactured sea water be placed in the open air and allowed to stand for "some time." Live algae should be added to the mixture, he goes on, as they will supply oxygen. The water should be filtered several times after the algae have been in it as this makes the water "still more fitted to receive animals." Place only the more hardy specimens in the mixture at first, he warns, and later on in the paper he states: "Like wine, salt-water, if properly treated, improves with age. . . ." He mentions that the water in the Hamburg Aquarium was not changed for fifteen years and at the end of that period it was still clear and odorless.

We have not found in other reports that salt water "improves with age," but the formula offered by Mr. Hoffman is not too different from others found in much later papers.

The formula given in *A Dictionary of Science* by Uvrarov and Chapman, 1954, a Penguin Reference Book, is as follows:

Water	96.4	Per cent
Common Salt	2.8	" "
Magnesium Chloride	0.4	" "
Magnesium Sulphate	0.2	" "
Calcium Sulphate	0.1	" "
Potassium Chloride	0.1	" "

Dr. Harvey, in his *Chemistry and Biology of Sea Water,* cited earlier in this chapter at the end of the section on pH control, credits Lyman & Fleming (1940) with the following formula as including all the major constituents of natural sea water:

Common Salt	$NaCl$		23.477 grams
Magnesium Chloride	$MgCl_2$		4.981 "
Sodium Sulphate	Na_2SO_4		3.917 "
Calcium Chloride	$CaCl_2$		1.102 "
Potassium Chloride	KCl		0.664 "
Sodium Bicarbonate	$NaHCO_3$		0.192 "
Potassium Bromide	KBr		0.096 "
Boric Acid	H_3BO_3		0.026 "
Strontium Chloride	$SrCl_2$		0.024 "
Sodium Fluoride	NaF		0.003 "
Water	H_2O	to	1000 "

Like the Berlin Aquarium back in the 1880s, the salt-water hobby has suffered because aquarists by and large have not had an available supply of salt water. The difficulty in securing natural sea water has held the hobby back for many years, but with the introduction of the various commercial synthetic salt-water formulas, the problem has been solved.

The aquarist who has a great deal of time for his hobby might very well experiment with the many available formulas and develop information invaluable to himself and his fellow aquarists. However, as most of us are not so fortunate as to have time for such study, we are content to allow the commercial manufacturers of salts to experiment for us, and profit from what they have learned by using the products they develop and pass along to us. To indicate that anyone can whip up a batch of salts that will support reef specimens would be poor advice. A source of chemicals that are sufficiently free from impurities would be difficult to find, and blundering with expensive specimens would prove both costly and discouraging.

The aquarist who is not going to use natural sea water can use one of the artificial salt-water mixtures or a salt-water concentrate. The first group covers the dry mixtures which are marketed under various trade names. The second, the salt-water concentrates, actually should not be classed as artificial formulas since they are, as their name implies, natural sea water from which a percentage of the water has been removed. The dissolved matter, however, is present; this is indicated by the high salinity readings they give when tested.

Of the dry mixtures on the market, Neptune Salts, a product of the Westchester Aquarium Supply Company of White Plains, New York, is probably the most widely used formula at this writing. It comes well packaged and the directions for its use are clearly written and easy to follow. Soon after the mixture has been added to tap water and dissolved, the solution is ready to receive specimens. Many aquarists who are using this formula give favorable reports on it and it certainly commands an important position in the hobby. One of the restrictions on the use of Neptune Salts is that it cannot be mixed with natural sea water. The reason for this seems to be based, insofar as we can determine, on the assumption that natural sea water cannot be maintained in good condition in a closed-system aquarium because of the minute life it contains, organisms from which Neptune in solution is free.

Of course, if Neptune Salts were mixed with fresh salt water, some of the minute marine life inherent in the latter would be included in the mixture. Undoubtedly, when mixed with tap water initially, Neptune or any of the dry mixes for that matter, contains little or no minute life, but just as soon as specimens are released in it, this is no longer true. After a tank of Neptune Salts, or any of the other synthetics, has been set up for a period, it seems to contain as much minute life as natural sea water. Dr. Harvey reports, however, that most bacteria found in sea water are not sustained by synthetic mixtures even when all the major constituents of natural sea water are included in the formula. This could be construed as a point in favor of all the salt mixtures, although some bacteria are certainly beneficial in breaking down waste products.

The different brands of salt mixtures have become numerous and we are not in a position to appraise them all individually. The directions for the use of some advise that a portion of natural sea water be added to the mixture. Others do not take up this question at all.

Public aquariums have been using one kind or another of the synthetics for many years, so there is no doubt that the various mixtures now offered to aquarists will support sea animals; for how long, has yet to be satisfactorily determined. Reliable longevity records have not been readily obtainable, probably because the hobby is so new. In the chapters on the various species of reef fishes, longevity records that have been well substantiated will be given.

We might also mention at this point the fact that only the major constituents of natural sea water are used in any of the synthetics; the trace elements found in the natural medium are missing. Whether the questionable claims to a low bacteria count and the absence of minute life outweigh the value of the missing trace elements is highly debatable. The ease of handling, shipping, and storing salt mixtures are advantages not to be discounted, however, and there is no question that herein lies their greatest value.

The salt-water concentrates which make up the second category of commercial salt water are certainly worthy of the aquarist's consideration. Eden Brine, marketed by the San Francisco Aquarium

Society, Inc., has received the most attention in this group. This medium, which is stored over a period of time before it reaches the aquarist, contains little or no minute life. This, plus the fact that it does have all the trace elements found in natural sea water, makes it highly acceptable. Although liquids are never as easily handled as dry materials, Eden Brine comes bottled in gallon jugs which are well packed in cartons. Like Neptune Salts, it can be used with tap water, but when water is lost through evaporation, distilled water is recommended for replacement to "avoid a further concentration of undesirable salts." The instructions that come with this product are thoughtfully written and easy to follow. From our own experience and that of other aquarists who have used Eden Brine, it has proved itself to be a highly successful medium for reef fishes.

To summarize an appraisal of the salt-water substitutes, from our own research and experimentation, we cannot rate them as being more satisfactory than natural sea water for aquarium use. We stress their value rather from the point of view that they are easier to handle and more accessible to the average aquarist. Those who live in thickly populated seaports would do well to use them rather than to chance water collected along shores which most certainly are contaminated by industrial waste products and filth. Unfortunately, the uninitiated in the hobby cannot comprehend the care that must be taken in collecting sea water in order to deliver it in condition suitable for the aquarium. Therefore, there is risk in securing water from fishermen or friends who go out several miles from shore in their boats. Unless the aquarist has access to lonely, unpopulated shores where the water rolls in from the open sea and is not diluted by rivers that are freighted with filth and pollution, he would do well to elect one of the commercial concentrates or mixes for aquarium use.

We have mentioned Neptune Salts and Eden Brine specifically only because at this writing they are best known in their respective categories.

Light and the Marine Aquarium

In many articles and pamphlets pertaining to marine aquarium maintenance, absence of sunlight is strongly advocated. This advice is given on the basis that "captured" sea water exposed to hours of sunlight is apt to turn green due to microscopic suspended algae that thrive under such conditions.

Water that is collected during the early spring or fall is more apt to react this way than water obtained in midsummer or winter. This is true because the ocean, like the land, is subject to seasonal changes. In the early spring, the growth of phytoplankton (plankton that consists of plants rather than microscopic animals) is stimulated by nutrients that have been resting on the ocean floor all winter but which are now surging upward because of a slow rise in the water temperature. The plant life, fed by nutrients that were not available in the winter, flourishes in the sunlight that penetrates the water to a limited depth, and a thriving crop results. Water collected during this period is very apt to turn green in the aquarium unless it is thoroughly filtered and stored for at least three weeks before using.

During the summer when the ocean reaches a fairly stable temperature, the plankton dies down and water collected during this period will not be apt to turn green. Filtration and storage are recommended anyway for a reduction of microscopic life and organic material.

Salt-water concentrates, artificial salt water, or well-processed natural water are not likely to turn green in strong sunlight. Some suspended algae in the water, however, are beneficial and, as we have mentioned before, algae that grow on the sides and rear wall of the aquarium should be encouraged. Not only is this plant life a factor in maintaining the pH in the proper range, but it cannot be surpassed as a diet supplement for fishes. Sunlight is necessary to support such growth. If the water seems to be developing suspended algae to the point of changing the color of the water, control is in order. Stepped-up filtration and subdued light for a day or two should be sufficient. Water that becomes completely out of hand should be filtered and stored, but under normal circumstances, with proper initial handling, this condition will not occur. Green water, aside from obscuring the fishes from view, is dangerous. If the suspended microscopic plants that cause it should suddenly begin to die off, the water would become foul. Green water that remains healthy, however, will not harm specimens, but because it is unsightly and is a potential hazard, the aquarist will do well to eliminate it. Never use chemicals to rid an aquarium of suspended algae, however. The method we have outlined above may seem time-consuming but chemicals strong enough to kill algae growth will prove toxic to specimens. Public and private exhibits of marine life have suffered great losses of valuable specimens through the use of chemicals.

Algae will grow on the sides and rear walls of aquariums in the presence of light even if artificial salts are used. Until such a condition is achieved, a vegetable diet from other sources must be supplied. This will be gone into more thoroughly in the section on feeding in Chapter 4. When tanks are lighted only by artificial light, some algae will develop but seldom will they thrive to the point that they can be depended on as the main source of vegetable fare for the specimens. Two 30-watt fluorescent tubes left on for about twelve to fourteen hours a day will give off enough light to promote some algal growth. Be sure the lights you select give off red rays for these are necessary for plant growth. Daylight and white tubes both give off red rays but Mazda bulbs give off considerably more.

Tanks that are constantly in artificial light should be watched for pH change. Such tanks tend to go acid, as explained under pH Control earlier in this chapter.

It is not wise to leave artificial lights on constantly to make up for the absence of sunlight. Fishes need a period of darkness, as do all living things.

Detection of Toxic Conditions in Marine Aquarium Water

It is difficult to determine whether or not a toxic condition exists in the salt-water aquarium. In most cases the change is not great enough to allow its detection by a pH reading. The specimens themselves serve as an indicator, but the symptoms they display when suffering from toxic water resemble very closely those of disease. Therefore a method of deduction must be employed in order to differentiate between toxicity and disease. At best this system is mostly trial and error. Even an experienced fish pathologist, examining a dead specimen, frequently cannot determine whether the parasites which are present were actually the cause of death, because of their rapid increase after the fish dies.

A toxic condition in aquarium water can develop slowly over a long period, or it can occur in twenty-four hours. We are assuming at this point that toxicity is present in the aquarium, and that the specimens were received from a source that was free from toxicity. When poison slowly seeps out of cement which is chemically unstable in salt water, it is often offset if the aquarist frequently changes the water. In a case of this type, it may be a long time before the aquarist becomes aware that a toxic condition exists in the tank. He may lose specimens from time to time but may charge the loss to the assumption that salt-water fishes are difficult to keep. After several such losses, he may conclude that the beautiful reef specimens are incapable of surviving aquarium conditions generally, and, without further thought, give up the hobby.

Actually, reef fishes are hardy if the aquarium conditions meet their rather fastidious requirements. Most of them have very long life spans when compared to those of fresh-water fishes, and adapt very well to confined aquarium conditions. This latter is probably due to the fact that they never wander very far from the sponge or coral they consider their particular territory when they are living in their natural environment. It is difficult for the aquarist, however, to accept these facts when he has just lost a beautiful specimen in a tank he considers to be perfectly "balanced." If it can be remembered that salt-water fishes (any living thing, for that matter) never "just dies," the aquarist will have come a long way. Old age is not a factor here because only very young specimens are available to hobbyists unless they deliberately seek out adults.

If specimens die after living in an aquarium for a few months, a building up of toxic conditions should be suspected unless new fishes have been introduced during that period. A specimen suffering from toxic water usually reveals its trouble by glancing off coral over and over again. At first it will eat readily and swim normally but from time to time it will scratch or bump against some rough surface for relief. Perhaps only one specimen will act in this way in the beginning, but as time goes on, the aquarist will notice that all the fishes in the aquarium are doing the same thing. If the condition is not corrected promptly, the fishes will begin to lose interest in food and their respiration will become rapid. Some fishes begin to lose color while others show no change until their fins begin to appear ragged. Because fishes also act in this way when they are attacked by parasites, it is now that the aquarist must try to determine whether or not toxicity is the cause of the trouble. If an aquarium that has been going along well for a few months begins to show signs that all is not well, and *no new specimens* have been introduced without first being placed in an isolation tank for fourteen days, the tank should be checked thoroughly for sources of toxicity.

Although these sources have been mentioned before, we shall go over them again briefly. Aquarium cement, breaking down under attack by salt water, will cause a chemical change in the water which can be toxic to fishes. Metal coming in contact with water may be the cause of the trouble; or corals that have been bleached by strong chemicals may be the source. Aquariums that have been treated indiscriminately with drugs may become toxic. Standard aquariums, the seams of which have been sealed off with asphalt, are completely unsatisfactory. Phenol is one of the toxic chemicals that is released into the water when asphalt is employed in this way.

If any of these conditions exist in the salt-water aquarium, the

John Hoke

Figure 11. French or black angelfish that has been subjected to toxic water.

aquarist can be sure that a chemical change is occurring in the water. Unfortunately the only way the aquarist can recognize the trouble is by the reaction of the specimens. pH tests fail to indicate the change because it is usually so slight that little or no difference appears in the reading. The water remains clear and odorless, and it is only through a series of deductions that the aquarist can discover the cause of the trouble.

Large public aquariums have had their troubles with toxicity. Accounts of such problems are given in papers written by the scientists who are in charge of these institutions. Great care is given to the types of material that are used to make up their equipment and costly changes are made when a source of toxicity is discovered. Unlike the home aquarist, however, they have the advantage of working with chemists who can analyze the water for them. An analysis of water can be a very expensive proposition for the hobbyist who generally works alone.

We have covered the sources of toxicity which have given us trouble in our experiments to enable the aquarist, through a careful rundown of the equipment he is using, to determine where he has gone wrong. When he has checked carefully and discovers any one of the sources we have mentioned, he should immediately transfer the specimens to uncontaminated water, using five-gallon, wide-mouthed jugs for temporary quarters if nothing else is available. Plenty of air should be supplied, for the jugs offer very little air surface. If the specimens are taken out of the contaminated water in time, there is a chance they may be saved. Removal to non-toxic water will give them relief and, unless they have been subjected to poisoned water too long, within a few hours they should be behaving normally.

If aquarium cement is suspected of being the source of the chemical upset in the water, another type of aquarium is in order. (See Chapter 2 on selecting a salt-water aquarium.) At this time a plastic tape is being developed which will protect aquarium water from standard aquarium cement when it is applied to the seams of the interior of the tank. This product will no doubt be on the market by the time this book is published. Articles and pamphlets that were written when the salt-water hobby was just becoming popular advocated the use of asphalt varnish, and later roofing asphaltum was recommended for this purpose. Both these materials have proved to be completely un-satisfactory. The varnish chips off in time, affording no protection at all, and, as we have said, the roofing asphaltum releases phenol into the water which is particularly deadly. Later, it was hoped that what are termed the *epoxies* in the field of plastics were the answer. Although they remain chemically stable in salt water, we have found that their quality of adherence is not satisfactory.

Whatever the cause of toxicity, it must be corrected before the fishes are returned to their tank. At this writing changing fishes to containers of uncontaminated water is the only treatment known for specimens that have been subjected to toxic water.

Collecting Natural Sea Water

We have already mentioned that natural sea water should be col-lected on margins of the open sea, away from thickly populated areas, and on an incoming tide. Water collected some way out from such an isolated shore is even better as its bacteria count will be less than that of shore water. This is true because bacteria breed in the silt on the ocean floor along the edges of the sea. The ocean floor where the water is deep has little or no bacteria.

The fact that water collected during the winter or summer will con-tain less microscopic life than that obtained during the early spring or fall, when vertical currents bring nutrients to the plankton and stim-ulate its growth, should not discourage the aquarist from collecting water in the spring or fall months. He should merely be alerted that water taken at these periods must be carefully filtered.

Equipment needed for a collecting trip can be kept down to a mini-mum if the activity at the seashore is to be confined to obtaining water for the aquarium. Containers for the amount of water required, of course, will have to be included. Each person who is going into the water should be equipped with a plastic bucket. If the water is to be filtered at the shore, plastic funnels and nylon or glass wool filtering material should be brought along. Collecting in winter necessitates the use of hip boots.

Either plastic bags or five-gallon jugs can be used as water containers. If jugs are used, vinyl plastic can be stretched over the tops and held in place by rubber bands.

When plastic bags are used, they should be tested for leakage before leaving for the seashore. One bag should be fitted into another as a precautionary measure against leakage. These bags are thin and frequently develop leaks. They should never be packed in metal drums or cans as the sharp edges of the seams of these containers rupture the water-filled plastic bags very easily and the water lost through leakage cannot be used because it has come in contact with metal. Both plastic bags and five-gallon glass jugs should be packed in corrugated cardboard cartons. Packed in this way either type of container can be safely shipped or transferred by automobile.

Plastic buckets are recommended for carrying water from the ocean to the shore because they are easily filled in an incoming tide. Further, their general pliability renders them especially useful in pouring water. They could be used as containers in the same way as the vinyl bags or five-gallon glass jugs are, as many types come equipped with plastic covers, but they are rather expensive.

When vinyl bags are used, a supply of soft cord should be taken along or plastic-covered wire to tie them up after they have been filled.

Filtering water at the shore can be done rather easily by pouring the water from the collecting bucket into a plastic funnel packed with the filtering material. The funnel, of course is either inserted into the mouth of a 5-gallon jug or is held by someone over a plastic bag that is supported by a corrugated carton. The task is a long and tedious one and should not be attempted unless the weather is pleasant.

Sometimes it is necessary to use newly collected water at once. This can be done, but the water should be filtered before pouring it into the aquarium. It is better not to mix newly collected sea water, even when it has been carefully filtered, with water that has been used in the aquarium for some time. If a change of water is necessary immediately, place the water that has been used in dark storage. It will be ready for service again in about three weeks. When old aquarium water is mixed with newly collected sea water, sometimes microscopic life is stimulated greatly and a biological unbalance occurs. If the newly collected sea water is not needed immediately, it should be placed in dark storage after it has been filtered.

Very often newly collected water appears cloudy. This is due to suspended material in it and does not mean that the water is contaminated. If the water has been collected on an isolated shore away from industrial and thickly populated areas, it is safe to use.

If the salinity of the water is less than is desired, a good grade of aquarium salt can be used to bring it up. Eden Brine, the salt-water concentrate, can also be used for this purpose.

CHAPTER 4

Suggestions for Keeping Salt-Water Fishes Healthy

Observations on the Physical Make-up of Salt-Water Fishes • Feeding • Causes of Deaths in the Salt-Water Aquarium • Symptoms of Disease and Treatment

Observations on the Physical Make-up of Salt-Water Fishes

As marine aquarists, we are chiefly interested in the study of salt-water *bony* fishes (the class Osteichthyes) because the specimens are select for our tanks come under that general category. The fishes included in this class have bony skeletons and usually a plate, called an operculum, covering the gill chamber. Figure 12 shows external parts of fish.

All fishes are vertebrates, or animals possessing backbones. Members of the class Chondrichthyes (*Elasmobranchii*), such as sharks and rays differ from the bony fishes in that their skeletons are cartilaginous rather than bony. All fishes, however, are usually streamlined, an adaptation to the medium in which they live; their fins are appendages designed for locomotion; and their tails, or caudal fins, are shaped to complement the rate of speed common to the various species.

The gills are the breathing organs of fishes. In the *bony* fishes they are made up of two chambers, one on either side of the pharynx which lies between the mouth and the oesophagus. Each chamber contains a series of gill filaments. The gill filaments are edged with

84

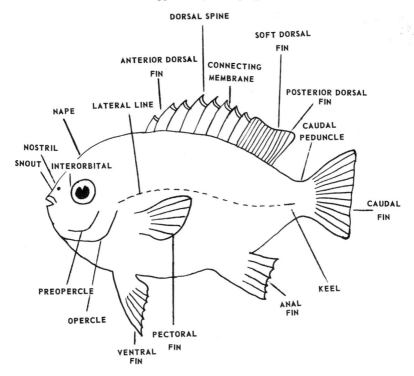

Figure 12. EXTERNAL PARTS OF FISH

leaflets so that the surface area of these fleshy projections is extensive. The gill chamber is covered with a thin plate, or operculum, that can be opened and shut. When the fish takes water into its mouth, the gill plates are pressed closed so that water flows into the gill chambers from the mouth only. The water is forced through the gill slits and released through the opening between the operculum and the body. In passing through the gill slits, the water bathes the gill filaments and leaflets and an interchange of gases is accomplished. Blood passing through the leaflets and filaments of the gills absorbs oxygen dissolved in the water and at the same time unloads the carbon dioxide in the blood (*see* Figure 13).

The heart and circulatory system work together in fishes in much

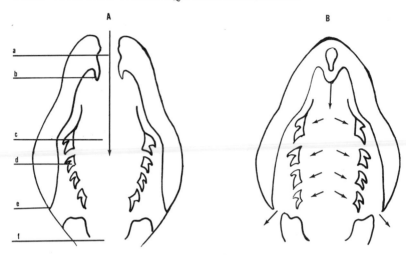

Figure 13. EXCHANGE OF GASES IN THE RESPIRATORY PROCESS

a Mouth; **b** Oral valve; **c** Pharynx; **d** Gill filaments; **e** Gillplate; **f** Esophagus.

    A shows open mouth and closed gill plates. Arrow indicates water flowing in mouth (**a**). Gill plates (**e**) are closed and water flows into pharynx (**c**).

    B shows mouth closed and gill plates open. Arrows indicate water bathing gill filaments (**d**). Oxygen is absorbed from the water by the filaments and carbon dioxide is released and carried off by the water through the open gill plates.

the same way as they do in mammals. The heart is the pump that circulates the blood to every part of the body. It is a one-circuit system, the blood leaving the heart and proceeding on to the gills to be relieved of carbon dioxide and to pick up new oxygen. It then travels to all the living cells of the fish, carrying oxygen with it. Processed food from the digestive system becomes suspended in the plasma and is carried to the muscles, nerves and organs by arteries. Here capillaries deliver the processed food and oxygen to cells where part of the food is oxidized and converted into energy, while some is used to build tissue. The waste products from both activities, water and carbon dioxide, are returned through capillary walls to the blood, to be received by the veins which carry the now impure blood back to the heart. Some waste chemicals are filtered through the kidneys before the impure blood reaches the heart but carbon dioxide is still present in the blood when the heart pumps it to the gills. Here it is released into the aquarium water, and fresh oxygen is taken on by the blood which is now completely relieved of waste material and ready to make the circuit again.

The physiological relationship of fresh- and salt-water fishes to the water in which they live differs considerably. This is due to what is termed *osmotic action*. Sea water is considerably more concentrated than the blood of a salt-water fish, whereas the blood of a fresh-water fish is denser than fresh water.

Although the coating of slime that covers a fish's body is almost waterproof, the blood of a fish is not completely out of contact with the water, for the gill membrane has to be permeable to allow the exchange of gases. Although it is permeable to water, it is not so to dissolved salts. When two solutions, one denser than the other, are separated by membrane, the solvent, or the weaker solution, moves into the denser one. This process is referred to as *osmosis*. Through this action, water from the salt-water fish's blood, a weaker solution than sea water, is constantly lost, and because water must be retained in order that the kidneys may function properly, replacement is always necessary. The fish, by drinking water, supplies fluid for the work of the kidneys. The excess salts are expelled through specialized cells in the gills and perhaps the roof of the mouth. If salt-water fishes were not highly specialized to offset this building up of salt content, they would become dehydrated, a condition that would be fatal.

The removal of slime in large areas of the fish's body through injury could cause dehydration, depending, of course, on the extent of the damage, for water would be lost faster than the fish could replace it. Likewise, if the salt-excreting cells in the gills were damaged by toxic conditions in the aquarium water, the expelling of excess salt could not be carried on and the specimen would eventually die.

A bony salt-water fish, therefore, must take on water constantly to replace that which is lost through osmotic action. Because dissolved salts are not passed through the gills (or membrane) in the process of osmosis, the fish not only has retained the salt of the water lost but gains additional salt from the water taken in for replacement. It is subject to the biological problem of taking on enough water to replace water lost through osmosis and excreting the accumulation of dissolved salts. The teleost, or bony salt-water fish, in order to conserve water, has a simplified kidney that does not perform the complex operations of filtration that the kidney of the fresh-water fish does. Although some excess salts are lost through the kidneys, the salt cells in the gills are depended upon for most of this work. A fish that is kept in water with a high salinity overtaxes its organs in ridding itself of salts. What under natural conditions is recognized as a biological disadvantage now becomes an unnatural burden. On the other had, a salt-water fish placed in fresh water takes on fluid which it is unable to expel. Unless it is returned to salt water in very short order it becomes waterlogged and eventually dies.

Salt-water bony fishes do adapt to gradual changes of salt concentration, however, and some are able to withstand an abrupt change without hardship. These are the fishes usually found in estuaries such as the killifishes and sticklebacks. They are equipped with the efficient kidneys of the fresh-water fishes and also possess the means of excreting excess salts. Most marine specimens, however, cannot withstand abrupt changes in salinity and cannot be converted to one hundred per cent fresh water.

The blood of a teleost fish consists of plasma containing red and white corpuscles along with smaller cells referred to as platelets. The red corpuscles carry oxygen throughout the body, while the white blood cells, which are considerably less in number than the red, protect the fish from infection. The platelets help to coagulate the blood when blood vessels are broken. The plasma contains many dissolved substances along with the blood cells and transports them throughout the body. Lymph, a diluted plasma, shuttles the oxygen from the blood to the tissues, bathes them, and carries off waste products of metabolism through the capillaries.

Fishes are endowed with the senses of touch, smell, taste, sight, and hearing. It is believed that a fish tastes with all of its body. Some fishes take nourishment from the water through the cells of their body as well as through their digestive systems. Fishes make sounds and it has been proved that some are aware of color. The temperature of a

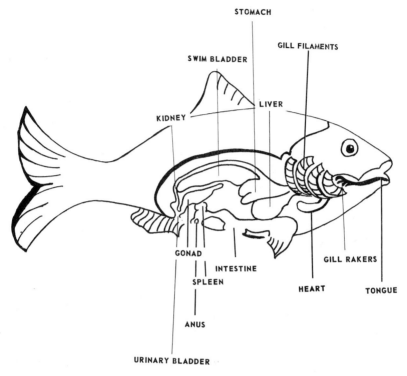

Figure 14. INTERNAL ORGANS

fish, due to heat produced by body chemistry, is slightly higher than that of the water around it. They are dependent on their environment for warmth as they do not possess the heat-regulating mechanism present in warm-blooded animals.

Most bony fishes possess an air-bladder. It usually lies above the stomach but under the backbone (*see* Figure 14). There has been much controversy as to its function but it is generally accepted that in some fishes it serves as an auxiliary source of oxygen. It also serves as a means of establishing equilibrium between the fish and the water. Sometimes a fish that is moved from one salinity to a more concentrated one will float until an adjustment of gas in the bladder is made. The air-bladder functions as a hearing device for many fishes and makes it possible for others to produce sound. By membrane or bony connections from the air-bladder to the inner ears, vibrations are relayed which have been picked up by the bladder. In some fishes the air bladder is connected to certain muscles. By rapid contractions of these muscles, the bladder vibrates and produces a drumming sound.

All fishes sleep and aquarium fishes are no exception. Fishes in the wild state have various sleeping habits. A hungry fish, however, that ordinarily sleeps when in darkness, will remain awake and active. Fishes that do not adjust well to aquarium conditions are often found swimming back and forth or up and down in the aquarium while its tankmates sleep in their favorite places. Such a specimen should be returned to the sea for it will not do well in captivity and its presence will upset other fishes that are otherwise well adjusted. Fierce battles are sometimes fought over a sleeping place. We once had a blue demoiselle that was docile and mild throughout the day. At dusk, however, this little specimen acquired another personality. It would industriously remove grains of sand from under a piece of coral. Other fishes, apparently accustomed to brushing it aside, would sometimes interfere with this activity. They were met with stiff resistance and driven away. When night finally settled down on the tank, the little blue demoiselle would be safely ensconced in the spot it had chosen for nocturnal retirement.

The brilliant colors of tropical fishes have been explained in several ways. Some writers claim that the bright colors serve as a means of protection in that they blend with the corals among which the fishes live. Others maintain that in tropical waters mutations are successful because of the "good living" conditions. Warm temperatures prevail, hiding places abound and food is always available in waters such as those off the Florida Keys. Whichever theory the aquarist accepts is secondary to his desire to maintain the varied colors of his specimens. The preservation of color and its connection with diet will be discussed further along in this chapter in the section on feeding. But there are other factors involved, the knowledge of which will be helpful to the aquarist.

The colors displayed by fishes are due to various colored pigment cells, or chromatophores, found in the dermal layer of the skin. Each cell is a sac with highly elastic walls, containing a granule of pigment. Because the cells are muscled and contain nerves connected to the spinal cord, they can expand and contract. A waste product excreted by the liver and pancreas called guanine, found in the skin, scales, bladder and the silver layer of the eye, is responsible for the iridescence some fishes possess. This crystalline substance may be surrounding the black-pigmented chromatophores, or crystals of guanine may occur as separate corpuscles. It sometimes forms a network of the entire body of the fish. The guanine corpuscles have no nerves.

A mixture of chromatophores, each containing a different pigment, either red, orange, yellow or black, make for the various colors of fishes. A fish with a black stripe is one that possesses a concentration of black chromatophores in that particular area.

The red to yellow chromatophores are fed by the vegetation the fish includes in its diet. Carotene is derived from algae; without this plant pigment, the chromatophores containing warm colors would soon pale out.

Color changes when they are of a permanent nature are alarming to the aquarist. They are associated with environment, food, reproduction, emotion and age; some are natural changes and others are due to questionable conditions. It has been ascertained that a light environment often causes fishes to pale out and that the change is directly connected with their ability to see. Many experiments have been designed to demonstrate the faculty of fishes to adapt in color to their environment, but this ability is definitely limited if the eyes are prevented from seeing. Thus a light or dark environment has a direct effect on the coloration of specimens. This was demonstrated to us quite clearly some time ago when an aquarist living out of the United States wrote us that fishes he had had shipped from the States lost their color soon after he introduced them to his very large and beautiful aquariums. He sent photographs of his tanks to us and we were greatly impressed by the many beautiful types of coral he had displayed in them. The photos were clear and the coral was brilliantly white. He continued to complain in his letters that his fishes were pale. The blues were faded, he told us, and the yellows were almost white. We went over his setup carefully. His feedings included vegetable matter and the fishes ate well. It finally occured to us that always in the photographs he sent us the coral appeared brilliantly white. We inquired into this and he admitted that he conscientiously scrubbed his coral once a month, removing any accumulated algae and bleaching out any stains that were present. He described the elaborate procedure he went through to purge the corals of the bleach before returning them to his aquariums. We suggested that he forgo the removal of the coral for a while. The last letter we had from him, although it did not contain any photographs, confirmed our suspicions. He had allowed the coral to become covered with algae and although he no longer had strikingly white coral, the fishes had regained their natural coloration, and he was more than pleased with the results. He was of the opinion now that his aquariums seemed more natural and he was content to allow the coral to become merely part of the background to complement his colorful specimens.

Fresh-water aquarists are well acquainted with the color changes that occur in specimens during breeding. This apparently is caused by the stimulation of hormone glands.

Salt-water aquarists soon become acquainted with changes due to emotional upset. Four-eyed butterfly fishes go through a series of color changes when they become frightened. Furthermore, these fishes pale out toward evening when they are ready to sleep.

Age affects the coloring of many specimens. Sometimes the color present in an adult fish differs from that of the young of the same species so much that unless the fish has been studied at close range by ichthyologists, it may be thought that the juvenile and adult are two different species.

The color changes that alarm the aquarist most, however, are the permanent ones that sometimes indicate that the fish concerned is not in good health. Most of the changes we have described are temporary in nature and are due to a shifting of the chromatophores which are closely connected to the nervous system of the fish. The change due to a diet deficiency is not included in this group, however, and the paling out will be permanent unless the diet is properly regulated. (See the section of this chapter on feeding.)

In black fishes, or fishes containing a great deal of black in their coloration, such as black or French angelfishes, sometimes the black fades to a muddy gray. If specimens are approaching maturity, this can be a natural change, but in young specimens it is a symptom that something is wrong. Unfortunately, we have seen it occur both in fishes subjected to toxic conditions and on other occasions in specimens infected with parasites. The fading out may be due to the fact that oxygen is being cut off from the cells as a result of gill infection or gill damage, and an insufficient amount is being carried throughout the body.

Any color change that persists and cannot be accounted for by the age of the fish or other natural causes, should be watched carefully. Very often it will eventually correct itself but occasionally it is followed by other signals that conditions are poor.

Feeding

It has been previously suggested that the aquarist specify small specimens when ordering. Fishes measuring a little over an inch from snout to tail are ideal. This would apply to all specimens, although length is not necessarily indicative of age. For instance, a clownfish (*Amphiprion percula*) an inch long would be an older fish than a black angel measuring the same. This discrepancy is accounted for by the ultimate size of the specimen. Black angelfishes are said to reach almost two feet in length when adult under natural conditions, whereas a clownfish might reach only four inches. Therefore, the growth of an angel is comparatively faster than that of a clown.

It is helpful for the aquarist to be able to approximate the age of his specimens because very young specimens require frequent feedings. Whenever possible, the adult size of fishes will be given in the chapters to follow on the various species to aid the aquarist in judging the approximate age of the specimen in question. Adult measurements, however, are deceptive for there is considerable evidence that a fish grows as long as it lives.

Small specimens are advocated because they adapt readily to aquarium conditions and feeding. A butterfly fish (*Chaetodon capistratus*) for instance, measuring from two and a half to four inches from head to tail, has already established eating habits in its natural habitat. It is often difficult to persuade this species to accept aquarium fare. A specimen of the same species measuring a little over an inch, usually settles down to aquarium life rather quickly and is no particular problem when it comes to feeding.

Although the clownfish that measures slightly over an inch is older than either the butterfly or angel of the same measurement, its disposition is such that the period of adjustment is not long. In fact, most clowns that are shipped into the United States have already been adjusted to aquarium conditions.

When young specimens of any species are obtained, frequent feedings are necessary. A portion of brine shrimp should be offered about four times a day. If such frequent feedings cannot be managed, the aquarist should offer larger portions but not more than the fishes can eat from day to day. As the specimens grow larger, the frequency of the feedings can be cut down. Clouds of brine shrimp should never be allowed to accumulate, however. If they persist after the specimens have taken their fill at the end of the day, they should be removed by filtration. A power filter will remove them very quickly.

Lettuce should be offered along with brine shrimp at least once a day, unless algae are present on the walls of the aquarium. Just as soon as the specimens accept tiny pieces of washed raw shrimp and beef, these foods should become a permanent part of the diet. Other types of protein food such as chopped earthworms may be offered. Brine shrimp should be included in the diet until beef and shrimp replace it entirely. This will not happen, however, until the specimens are well on the way to adulthood.

Because brine shrimp, tiny pieces of washed shrimp and beef, and lettuce or algae have successfully maintained salt-water specimens, they should form the essential base of the diet. Prepared dried foods are accepted by specimens and make a fine supplement to the basic diet. Commercial dried foods that contain antibiotics of any description, however, should not be used. Any other foods should be treated as experimental and only offered in addition to the fare we have outlined.

The importance of vegetable matter in the diet of marine fishes is too often forgotten in articles and papers on the subject. Its importance will be mentioned again in the section of this chapter on disease. A natural source of such food is the algae that grow on the walls of the aquarium. We have introduced into our tanks French angels that had been in aquariums where algae were not present, and within the hour of their introduction to their new home they have cleaned away sections of growth from the walls and corals. In our experience, only a few marine animals we have kept have seemed to be completely carnivorous. Craig Phillips in his article on marine plants, previously mentioned in Chapter 2, inadvertently brings out the need salt-water fishes have for vegetable matter when he states: "One difficulty in maintaining these plants in the aquarium is the fact that a number of marine fishes will nibble at them. The worst offenders appear to be young angelfishes, butterfly fishes and surgeon fishes. . . ."

When algae are absent from the aquarium, as they will be in tanks that have only recently been set up, lettuce can be used as a substitute. Tiny pieces should be prepared and included in the initial feeding of new specimens although, at first, it may be refused. Within a few feedings, however, it is eagerly accepted and relished. French angels will take it from your fingers and clownfish will race and snatch the sinking pieces. Be sure the pieces are tiny enough for the specimens to handle. Tiny pieces of raw carrot may also be offered.

Tubifex worms should be excluded from the salt-water aquarium. Recently the value of tubifex worms has been questioned even in the diet of fresh-water fishes. Although the bacteria that accompanies tubifex may very well perish in salt water, the chance that some types may survive should not be taken and, as the foods we have named above unquestionably possess nutritional value, the need for tubifex is completely eliminated. Frozen daphnia and frozen brine shrimp are questionable as to actual food value and fall into the class of foods that should not be relied upon.

There are some types of marine fishes that want live food larger than brine shrimp and aquarists report that they cannot be coaxed into accepting raw beef and shrimp. Sea horses (other than the dwarf variety) are included in this group along with the lionfish (*Pterois volitans* and *Pterois radiata*). Aquarists living near the sea are able to supply such marine pets with tiny shrimp that are found in floating clumps of seaweed. Others not so fortunate must supply their pets with baby guppies. Better to cross these species that require small young fry off your list, however, if supplying such food is distasteful to you.

Hatching batches of brine shrimp in the necessary quantities is not a difficult chore. A flat Pyrex baking dish about three and a half inches deep with a two-quart capacity can serve as a container. Three table-spoons of aquarium salt to two quarts of water will give you the proper salinity. An air line should be placed in the solution and a little less than a half teaspoon of the eggs added to the water. A gallon jug can be used for the purpose also, but one with a wide mouth is necessary. Most brands of brine shrimp are satisfactory. Those sold by the San Francisco Aquarium Society are especially good. Brine-shrimp eggs should be kept in a dry place in an airtight container. Brine-shrimp eggs that have absorbed quantities of moisture will not hatch. Hatch-ings have been gotten from eggs that have been kept properly two years after they were first placed in storage.

There are various other methods of hatching brine shrimp. Hatchers have appeared on the market designed especially for this chore which probably have some merit. However, the method we have described has proved perfectly satisfactory.

It takes about twenty-four hours to hatch a quantity of eggs. The freshly hatched shrimp are removed from the container with a dip tube and caught in a small net made of fine nylon jersey material. When the water has drained away, the net containing the shrimp is dipped into the tank. Fishes that are most particular in their food tastes seem to relish this type of food and it has proved to be most satisfactory for all species of marine fishes. When specimens attain a growth of from four to five inches from nose to tail, brine shrimp sometimes are over-looked for small pieces of shrimp and lean beef.

Causes of Deaths in the Salt-Water Aquarium

There is no central source of information on diseases that attack aquarium fishes. Bird and animal fanciers are more fortunate in this respect since much work has been done in their fields. Even in the long-established fresh-water hobby only sketchy information regard-ing diseases of fresh-water tropicals has been gathered over a sub-stantial number of years. As breeders of these types of fishes are apt to regard their findings as trade secrets, it has been the aquarists themselves, some of whom have scientific backgrounds, who have passed along information regarding treatment to beginners in the field through books and magazine articles. Little or no information has been collected on treatment of diseases of salt-water tropicals, as the hobby is still in its infancy.

The exhibitors of salt-water fishes are often private organizations that operate on a profit-making basis and do not publish papers on their findings. Recently curators of public exhibits have been writing articles on phases of disease because increased interest in the salt-water field has given them an audience. Such welcome material is still rather rare, however, and has not yet become a vast source of information of the type that is available to the fresh-water hobbyist.

Fortunately, most salt-water specimens do not die of disease but are lost through other causes that are relatively easier to control. In a list of causes of deaths occurring in salt-water aquariums in order of frequency, it would be difficult to place the disease factor in its correct sequence. We have mentioned many times that toxicity is probably the most common cause of death in the home aquarium. Although malnutrition, injuries sustained through fighting and handling, maladjustments to aquarium conditions, and jumping out of the tank all take a considerable toll, the disease factor is so often governed by one or a combination of these that it becomes difficult to determine which actually came first, the disease or one of the factors we have outlined. And because the symptoms of toxicity are often so similar to those of disease, the latter is often suspected when actually toxicity is the trouble. If, however, the aquarist has eliminated the chances of toxicity by careful selection of equipment and supplies, his ability to diagnose disease is made comparatively simple.

As losses due to malnutrition, injuries and maladjustment can be prevented rather simply, we shall give these causes of death our first attention.

Proper diet not only serves as a prophylactic measure against infections and disease, but it enhances the beauty of specimens. A fish that is deprived of vegetation in its diet soon loses color. Yellows, oranges and reds are kept high and bright by a substance known as carotene which specimens derive from the vegetation they eat. If vegetable matter is lacking in the diet, the chromatophores containing yellows to reds pale out and the bright warm coloration of the specimen is lost.

Malnutrition often occurs when specimens are selected because of their particular interest to the hobbyist rather than for their adaptability to aquarium conditions. Members of the Chaetodon family are often lost because the aquarist has selected large specimens which measure three inches or more from head to tail, or are beyond the age when they adapt easily to a new environment and accept food to which they are not accustomed. Smaller specimens of this family accept food readily and continue to do so as they grow older because they have adjusted to unnatural aquarium conditions.

Small angels, specimens measuring less than an inch from head to tail, often starve to death in the aquarium, because fishes this small require several feedings of brine shrimp a day. If such feedings are offered, they thrive and grow fast.

Sea horses often refuse food if they are disturbed by other specimens. All sea horses should be kept in a tank by themselves. Most of them will refuse anything but live food.

When the aquarist has investigated the personality traits of the various species before he purchases his collection of fishes, he will save himself many losses.

Superficial injuries are open invitations to disease, for through them the protective slime on the surface of fishes is removed, giving a foothold to fungus and bacteria. Most injuries that occur in the aquarium are inflicted directly or indirectly by tank bullies. Sometimes pugnacious traits are peculiar to an individual of a species. Acquainting himself with the personality traits of a species will not help the aquarist in this instance. More often, however, quarrelsomeness is the characteristic of a species in general. If such a species is especially attractive to the aquarist, he should provide a separate tank for one or two specimens. In this way the rest of the peaceful members of his collection will be saved from wounds and scrapes sustained by brushing against coral in an attempt to avoid the bully.

Careful handling of fishes will eliminate injuries that occur when fishes are caught. The use of a glass bowl rather than a net when feasible will save the removal of slime from the body of the fish which often occurs when coarse netting material is rubbed or dragged against it. If a net must be used, gentleness and patience should be exercised in catching the fish. Removing coral from the aquarium saves the fish from colliding with it in its effort to escape the net.

Never drop a fish into a tank from a net held one or two feet over it. It seems unnecessary to mention this, but we have seen collectors who considered themselves tops in their field do this apparently without considering the fact that water is as hard as cement when hit by a flat surface.

In tanks that are overcrowded, fighting among specimens occurs even among ordinarily peaceful fishes. A tank should be large enough to provide coral refuges for each specimen. We would not recommend more than four small specimens to a fifteen-gallon aquarium.

High salinity seems to have a direct bearing on the disposition of fishes. We know that metabolitic rates run high in densities over 1.025. The fishes in this density eat more, become more active and are generally more irritable. (See the section on salinity control in Chapter 3.) Readings of 1.020 to 1.022 seem to tone down the general activity of fishes.

Some species of fishes do not respond well to aquarium life. These species are often listed in dealers' catalogues because they are attractive. Some of these, in natural conditions, are travelers. They form schools which often consist of several different species, and roam from place to place in search of food. In the aquarium they pace back and forth, upsetting the more tranquil members, unable to forget their roving habits. Others languish in captivity, refusing food and finally becoming the victims of malnutrition and disease. These types will be mentioned in the chapters devoted to the personality traits of fishes.

Losses sustained through fishes' jumping out of tanks can easily be corrected by keeping the aquarium covered at all times. Some fishes jump when they are startled. Occasionally they will leap if they are bothered by a bully. Whatever the reason may be, however, a cover will save specimens as well as keep foreign matter such as dust out of the aquarium.

Disease is often connected with some of the losses we have mentioned, but in these instances it comes as a result of wounds or conditions rather than as a direct cause of death. All of these types of losses are secondary in number to those caused by toxicity which, as we have mentioned before, takes the greatest toll of all.

Symptoms of Disease and Treatment

Unfortunately, the symptoms of disease or parasites resemble those of toxicity so closely that it is only after a series of deductions that the aquarist can distinguish one from the other.

Fishes manifest discomfort caused by disease or toxicity in several ways. The irritant affects the gills and the slime coating of the surface of the fishes and causes them to glance off corals, sand on the floor of the aquarium, or any other rough surface that is available. If either disease or toxicity is present, the specimens will react in this way. Actually, this unnatural kind of movement is scratching. Specimens will often appeal to one another for help by sidling up in a peculiar way to any of their tankmates. The novice might mistake this mannerism for playfulness or even as an initial gesture of courtship. Some specimens will actually oblige by nipping the infected fish. If the condition is not corrected, eventually all of the fishes will appeal to one another for help and show general distress. Often they will brush up against the appendages of hermit crabs to relieve what appears to be an itching sensation. Their surfaces become so sensitive that they sometimes avoid contact with brine shrimp. If specimens continually glance off corals or other rough surfaces as we have described, either a toxic condition exists in the aquarium or parasites are present.

The rate of respiration, or breathing, becomes rapid after a while. This, too, can indicate either the presence of toxic conditions or parasites. If the trouble is caused by toxicity, the irritant in the water permeates the slime coating on the gill filaments, causing it to harden. The membrane tissue is no longer permeable to gases and therefore the source of oxygen is gradually shut off. In the case of parasites, the rapid respiration is due to their becoming lodged in the gill filaments, and again the source of oxygen is cut down. When the damage becomes acute from either cause, the specimens will gasp at the water's surface in an effort to get the oxygen which is being denied them. When they have reached this stage, death will soon follow.

Discoloration can occur as a result of toxic conditions. The slime coating on the surface of the fish has been attacked, and a change of color occurs. Parasites also attack the slime coating, producing a change in the color of the specimen. However, here there is a difference in the effect of toxicity and parasites. If the discoloration is not uniform, or if the specimens seem to be covered with a dust or powder, the aquarist can be sure that parasites are present.

Loss of appetite seems to be a symptom that occurs only after the specimens have been damaged considerably by the cause of their disorder. It develops when the specimens are in the last stages of their fight for life and in no way would indicate whether they suffer from parasites or toxicity.

All of these symptoms are manifestations of disease or toxicity. In only one instance is there a difference in the appearance of the specimens. The aquarist can test for toxicity when trouble is first discovered by transferring all of the specimens to five-gallon glass jugs, well aired and filled with newly collected sea water, newly mixed concentrate, or synthetic salts. If the specimens show relief after a few hours have elapsed, it can be inferred that toxicity is the cause of the trouble. The contaminated water should be discarded and when the source of the toxicity is discovered, the correction should be made.

If, however, the transfer does not give any relief to the specimens and they continue to behave abnormally, parasites can be suspected as being the cause of the trouble.

In the case of salt-water parasites, we have found that treating the aquarium as a whole is the best method rather than taking specimens out one at a time and treating them separately in hospital tanks. Mei Lan of Oakland, California, a company we have previously mentioned, puts out a stock solution of copper sulfate which they call "Super Remedy." We have found that one teaspoon of this solution to three gallons of water will effect a cure. This is less than the directions suggest, but we have used it successfully at this strength in a severe case of *Oödinium ocellatum* and feel that cutting down the amount is wise.

Oödinium ocellatum is a parasite that attaches itself to the gill filaments and bodies of salt-water fishes. It can be seen by the naked eye if the available light is sufficient, and resembles a light sprinkling of gold dust over the body of the fish. The gill filaments of dead fishes have been found so profusely implanted by this parasite that impaired respiration was believed to be the cause of death. One specimen infected with these parasites can cause a major epidemic in an otherwise healthy aquarium as they multiply and spread rapidly. This is, of course, one of the reasons for the practice of isolating recently acquired fishes for a period of at least two weeks. Accounts of *Oödinium ocellatum* infecting populations of fishes in public aquariums as well as in privately maintained exhibits are fairly common in scientific literature and they might well be regarded as one of the most dangerous parasites to aquarium fishes.

Robert P. Dempster of the Steinhart Aquarium in San Francisco has written a very fine paper on the use of copper sulfate in combating parasites in the May, 1956, issue of the *Aquarium Journal.* In his paper he advises against using copper sulfate in a tank containing sand, gravel, coral, shells and so forth, if the aquarist is treating a collection of infected fishes. This is because the copper will become bound to the carbonates resulting from the coral, shells or gravel and some of it will be pulled out of solution, thus becoming ineffective. Corals and shells should be boiled and cleaned of algae that may be growing on them before they are returned to the aquarium.

Copper sulfate has been used as a preventive against parasites in many public and private exhibits. It is considered to be an effective weapon against any of the external parasites with the exceptions of flukes, leeches, and anchor worms, that attach themselves to marine specimens. It causes the fishes, according to Mr. Dempster, to secrete a copious amount of mucus which detaches the parasites. As long as this mucus is present on the fishes, the parasites are unable to cling to them. In instances of *Oödinium ocellatum,* when the parasites are no longer able to remain on the specimens, they fall to the bottom of the tank and cell division occurs. Before they are able to complete their cycle and become free-swimming dinoflagellates, which is the infective form, they are killed by the copper sulfate.

When the hobbyist discovers his aquarium is infected with parasites, he should treat the aquarium proper, rather than removing the fishes to isolation tanks. This will clear the water of parasites that are in other than infective forms. Water that has been treated can be kept in service. No tank, however, should ever be treated again with copper unless it has been tested for copper content. A copper kit can be purchased for this purpose and the amount of copper remaining in the water determined. This metal in large quantities is deadly to fishes. After a period of several months it is said to dissipate, but the aquarist should not rely on this assumption and add more copper to his aquarium without testing it first.

Although we feel that the hobbyist will do well to purchase a stock solution such as "Super Remedy," which we have mentioned, he can make his own stock solution of copper sulfate if he is unable to find this product on his dealer's shelf and doesn't have time to send away for the remedy. Mr. Dempster gives the following formula:

> 1 gram of copper sulfate chemically pure and carefully weighed to 1 liter of distilled water and stir with glass rod until it is completely dissolved.

> This solution will contain 1 milligram of copper sulfate in each milliliter.

> 7.43 milliliters should be used to each gallon of water.

Often aquarists do not have the equipment to make measurements such as those given in Mr. Dempster's paper. The hobbyist might take the above formula to his druggist and have him mix it for him, if this happens to be the case. The amount, 7.43 milliliters, given in the directions as the amount which is added to each gallon in the aquarium, is a little less than two teaspoonfuls.

Be sure that you know the exact number of gallons your tank holds and make sure that your measurements are accurate. To determine the exact capacity of your aquarium, the following formula may be used:

> Multiply the length by the height (in inches) of the aquarium and multiply this figure by the width (front to back measurement). Use *inside* measurements only. Divide this figure by 231. This will give you the number of gallons your aquarium actually holds.

Remember, when considering the gallonage of your aquarium, that displacement of water by coral, shells and sand should be accounted for, unless, of course, they are to be removed during treatment as they should be. When copper sulfate is being introduced into the aquarium as a preventive measure only and the corals and shells are to remain, displacement of water should be considered by all means. Aeration should be continued throughout treatment but filtration interrupted until it is no longer necessary to maintain the initial strength of the solution (when parasites have been destroyed). Aeration and filtration both should be used if medication has been used as a preventive measure only. In other words, coral and shells tend to weaken the copper solution. Filtration also gradually weakens the concentration. When full dosage is necessary in order to combat parasites, corals, shells and sand should be removed from the aquarium and filtration should be temporarily interrupted.

We have mentioned previously that species vary in their tolerance to toxicity. As copper sulfate is toxic, specimens vary in their reaction to it. When under treatment, specimens breathe faster but the actual rate of respiration differs among species. The following fishes have been subjected to copper sulfate and have subsequently showed no harmful effects due to the treatment:

French or black angelfish	Clownfish (*A. percula*)
High hat	*Dasycllus trimaculatus*
Cardinal	Dwarf sea horse
Neon goby	*Heniochus acuminatus*
Rock beauty	Blue demoiselle

In our opinion, most of the popular marine fishes now available to aquarists may be treated with copper sulfate. The only fish we have reason to question as to its tolerance to the medication is the four-eyed butterfly. Our data on the reaction of this particular species to copper sulfate is not complete enough to say more than that its tolerance is questionable.

We are suspicious of all cure-alls as a rule, but in our experience, copper sulfate is the best weapon against parasites that attack salt-water specimens. We cannot, however, recommend it as a fungicide or a cure for bacterial diseases. It is ineffective against parasites such as flukes, leeches and anchor worms, as we have pointed out previously.

When fungus appears on specimens, it is often due to injuries received in handling or sustained through quarreling. A fresh-water treatment may be given when the growth is first noticed. A clean, enameled pan should be filled with aged fresh water that is the same temperature as the water in the aquarium from which the patient is to be removed. The fish should be released into the fresh water and watched carefully until it shows signs of distress by blowing at the top or lying on the bottom of the pan. At this moment it should be transferred back into its home aquarium. If the patient, however, has been bullied and chased by a tankmate, some arrangement should be made so that the fish does not become victimized again. Either remove the bully and confine it to an isolation tank, or place the injured fish in a similar confinement until it recuperates and can again take its place in the aquarium community.

The fresh-water treatment is based on the theory that a fungus that forms in salt water cannot survive in fresh. This does not always hold true, however, and sometimes the area of the fish infected with fungus must be treated. Lilly's tincture of Merthiolate swabbed on the spot with a glass rod sometimes is effective. The fish should be held in a net with its head submerged in water if possible, while the medication is being applied. If the fungus is still present in a day or two, the treatment should be repeated. If the fungus still persists, the patient should be removed to the isolation tank. Aureomycin at the rate of one-half gram to a gallon, or 500 milligrams per gallon, should be introduced. Mix the drug with a portion of the aquarium water removed from the hospital tank first and then mix it with the water in the hospital tank. No further dosage should be given and the fish should be returned to the aquarium proper when a cure has been effected.

Caudal and pectoral fins that have ragged edges from tail and fin rot should be trimmed with scissors, the raw edges then painted with Lilly's tincture of Merthiolate.

Antibiotics should never be introduced into an aquarium as a preventive measure, nor should they be included in dry food. Any commercial food containing aureomycin or any other antibiotic should not be used, as there has been a preponderence of evidence that such additives retard rather than promote growth in fishes.

Suggested Reading

Brian Curtis, *The Life Story of the Fish,* New York, 1949
J. R. Norman, *A History of Fishes,* London, 1931
Charles K. Wichert, *Anatomy of the Chordates,* New York, 1951

CHAPTER 5

Collecting Specimens

*Planning the Collecting Trip · What to Take
Along on a Collecting Trip · The Hazards of
Collecting · The Art of Collecting · Conservation · Collecting Coral, Shells and Sand · Collecting Crabs, Anemones and Shrimp · Summary*

Planning the Collecting Trip

THE collection of specimens is always an exciting experience and
hobbyists often plan their vacations around just such a colorful adventure. Either a trip north to the coast of Maine, or south to the
Florida Keys can be filled with interest to the marine aquarist; for
every mile of seacoast holds its own particular store of fascinating
marine life.

We have devoted much of this book to the care of tropical marine
fishes because they are considered the most popular of the salt-water
specimens, and their maintenance demands highly specialized conditions. There are many hobbyists, however, who confine their interest to the little fishes and invertebrates found in estuaries and
northern waters and feel that this phase of the hobby is most satisfying because, although these creatures are not as colorful as the reef
fishes, they are fully as interesting and, as an additional attribute,
their requirements are not as exacting.

The maintenance of marine specimens, as we have mentioned before, has many phases. One aquarist may fancy the grotesque and
unusual, whereas another may choose only the colorful specimens.

We know many hobbyists who especially like the invertebrates and anemones and devote their entire aquarium space to these creatures.

Collecting, too, can be broken down into particular phases. The kinds of specimens one finds interesting may determine the locale of the collecting site. If time doesn't permit the aquarist to go to the place of his choice, however, a pleasant holiday can be spent collecting specimens that are fascinating but have no place in the aquarium, such as fiddler crabs, jellyfishes of the comb jelly varieties and sea slugs. A few books taken along to aid in the identification of marine life can add much interest to such a venture. Rachel Carson's *The Edge of the Sea* and N. J. Berrill's *The Living Tide* (now available in a paperback edition) are both excellent. Be sure, however, that the book you choose as a field reference covers the area where you intend to do your collecting.

Most collecting trips are made by car, although we have known hobbyists who have used public transportation, which, of course, reduces to a bare minimum the amount of equipment that can be taken along. Transportation by private automobile is by far the most practical mode of travel for most of us, however, and if space and weight are considered carefully, all the necessary equipment can be easily accommodated in a family car.

The most successful trips are carefully planned. If fishes are to be collected for the home aquarium, certain items of equipment are necessary and these should be listed and acquired.

The collecting site should be decided upon and reservations made for the vacation headquarters. Of course, one can just start out to a general destination and find a suitable place to make headquarters. However, an ideal location recommended by other collectors should be given some thought. Proximity to the water, availability of skiffs, electric outlets that can be used for pumps, all are necessary features of a successful collecting base. We go to the little town of Islamorada on the Florida Keys. Here we are sure of a clean little cabin on a beach facing the Atlantic. We rent it from Syd and Pat Beards who run a motel-type establishment called The Castaways. We like our little cabin especially because not only does its location give us lovely natural surroundings but it is particularly convenient for loading and unloading our boat. Nearby is a pleasant but not too fancy restaurant.

All in all, we have found a collecting site that fills our particular needs.

On the other hand, although you can save time by knowing exactly where you intend to stay, there is a kind of adventure attached to finding what you consider an ideal spot, and certainly there are many up and down the coasts of both the Atlantic and the Pacific.

If side trips or visits are to be made, it is better to plan these stopovers on the way to the collecting site rather than on the journey home when it is likely you will be anxious to get your fishes settled in their new home as soon as possible.

What to Take Along on a Collecting Trip

Regardless of which types of fishes the aquarist has in mind, if he plans to collect his specimens himself, he must be equipped with a certain amount of gear. As is true with all hobbies, the equipment can be elaborate and costly; but for the aquarist who wishes to keep costs down to a minimum, much of it can be homemade and relatively inexpensive.

When possible, in describing items of accouterment necessary for a collecting venture, we shall mention them in the order of their importance. Since methods of catching fishes differ according to the area chosen for the collecting site, the various types of gear used will be described as we go along.

No matter where the aquarist decides to collect, if he is planning to bring back a number of specimens for his aquarium, he must have facilities for aeration in his car. Any standard pump can be used but it must be equipped with a DC as well as an AC motor. These motors can be easily made interchangeable so that the DC motor is used while traveling in the car, and the AC motor is run at night while staying at a motel. The prudent aquarist will take a spare of each type of motor in case one of them burns out. It is very difficult to secure small electric motors while traveling or staying at an out-of-the-way place.

Enough vinyl tubing should be taken along so that the fishes can be aerated in jugs left in the car at night. The pump can be powered from an outlet in the motel room and the tubing run from the pump to the car. Tee connections should be included, as well as airstones and valves, so that the number of jugs that the collector intends to use for specimens can be accommodated.

The car should be parked close to the motel chosen for an overnight stop, so that the vinyl tubing can run from the room to the car and be hung out of the way of anyone walking by. Of course, the jugs can be carried into the motel (and should be if the weather is cold or changeable), but leaving them in the car saves considerable energy.

Motel managers are usually willing to allow collectors the use of electric power available in their establishments but it is a good idea to secure permission for the privelege before checking in.

The number of jugs necessary varies, depending on the number of specimens desired. If water for aquarium use is to be collected, containers will be necessary, of course, and either jugs or plastic bags can be used. If jugs are capped, be sure the metal is covered by either layers of wax paper or vinyl (the type used for shower curtains or clear tablecloths).

It is surprising how well fishes travel if proper aeration is provided. We have taken specimens with us on vacation trips at times when we had no one at home to give them proper care. Four clowns and two *Dascyllus* journeyed with us almost 3,000 miles and were none the worse for wear when they were returned to their home aquarium.

Temperature isn't a problem while traveling in the summer but winter travel necessitates insulated containers and a heated car. The jugs must be taken into the motel at night when temperatures are cold or changes are extreme.

While traveling, jugs containing fishes should be covered at all times to protect them from fumes and smoke. This is a safeguard, too, against their jumping out when startled. A bicycle pump can be taken along in case the electric pump breaks down so that the jugs can be aerated manually until the pump is put back into service. A plastic or Pyrex baster (the type with a bulb on one end) makes a temporary aerating device also.

The DC motor can be wired to a cigarette lighter in the car or included in the electric system by some other means. We have found that even while traveling at night this additional load on the battery is not enough to cause trouble.

Collecting in Florida waters is usually accomplished by working under water in depths that are seldom over one's head. The collector swims along in the water, looking down through his face mask for a sponge or bed of low-growing corals. When he spots a place which may possibly be the home of likely specimens, he gets to his feet, disturbing the area as little as possible. He either squats or bends from the waist, submerging his face into the water so that he can study the place of interest. This type of observation cannot be conveniently made without the aid of a face mask. One that doesn't fit properly is of little use as it allows water to leak in, which clouds the glass and makes vision impossible. A snug-fitting (yet comfortable) face mask is probably one of the most used items in the collector's gear. Expensive masks are not always the most satisfactory. Trying on the mask over the face before purchasing it and testing it by exhaling through the nose will insure good fit. If air escapes where the mask presses against the facial contours, it is better to try another one. When a mask fits properly, exhaling through the nose isn't possible. The type of mask that has one or two snorkels extending from the frame allows the collector more time under water. He is able to swim about a foot under water for long distances, his air coming to him from the snorkels, the openings of which are out of water. When he wants to descend to the ocean floor, the openings of the snorkels close as he heads downward, preventing water from flooding into his mask. From now on, he must hold his breath until he again ascends and the snorkels of the mask break the surface of the water. Although this piece of equipment is not essential for successful collecting, it does without a doubt enhance the experience of underwater swimming.

Nets are important tools in any type of collecting. Probably homemade ones are the most satisfactory. The frame of the net can be made of tubular aluminum and it should be shaped like a wide, closed letter U, the handle fitting into the curved part of the U (*see* Figure 15). This shape enables the collector to drag or push the straight edge of the net along the ocean floor when necessary, thereby preventing a way of escape for the quarry.

The handle should be about a foot long, or the length best suited for comfortable handling. The frame of the net should be covered with fairly fine mesh as some of the specimens to be caught are quite small. Rayon or cotton material can be used (*see* Figure 16). Nylon is rather

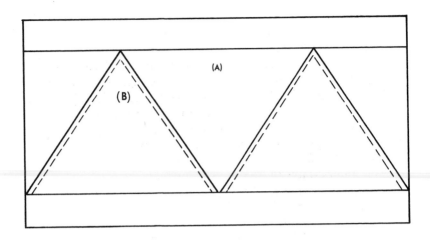

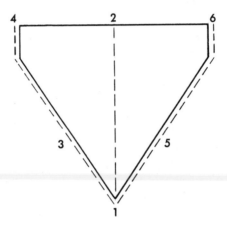

Figure 15. A PATTERN FOR TWO NETS

Two nets can be made from one piece of cotton or rayon curtain material measuring 3 feet by 6 feet.

The upper sketch illustrates the material spread out. The dotted lines indicate how the cloth is cut.

The lower sketch shows the shape of the net when seams are sewn. The dotted line from 1 to 2 represents the net designated as (**A**) of the upper sketch. The dotted line from 3 to 4 and 5 to 6 represents the seams of net designated as (**B**) of the upper sketch.

When seams are sewn, net will be sewn on frame (*see* Figure 16). This operation is best accomplished by hand.

hard and rough in texture and in the skirmish of catching a fish, it often rubs off some of the protective slime coating of the specimen. Each collector should have his own net. Some hobbyists may like to work with two, but one is usually adequate. A small aquarium dip net should be included in the equipment to be used when transferring fishes from one jug to another, which is sometimes necessary.

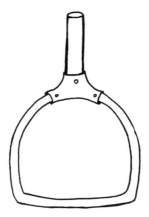

Figure 16. FRAME FOR NET

Frame can be made of tubular aluminum. Figure 15 shows how a piece of material can be cut to make two nets. This pattern is designed for a piece of material measuring 6 feet by 3 feet. If this pattern is used, a 6-foot length of tube should be used.

A seine is a good item to take along as it can prove very useful in some types of collecting. A small one about fifteen feet by four with small mesh will be easier to handle than the larger types that are not designed for a collector's use.

The collector should have a pair of sneakers. Treading over the ocean floor in bare feet is both uncomfortable and dangerous. Contact with sharp pieces of live coral can inflict wounds in the feet and sea urchins often lurk where one least expects them. Canvas shoes with toes out are not desirable for obvious reasons.

Polaroid sun glasses to protect the eyes from reflection and sun helmets or straw hats to shield the head from the tropical sun are essentials. They are standard equipment with the natives who have had a far better opportunity to build a resistance to both reflection and sun than the hobbyist who in most instances spends most of his time indoors or in a climate where the heat of the sun is not as intense or constant as it is in the tropics. Work gloves are good to have along for handling sponges and corals, contact with which sometimes affects the skin somewhat the way poison ivy does.

Containers have already been mentioned briefly. They are very important items, however, and should be considered carefully. Five-gallon jugs should be used as tanks in your vacation quarters and later as shipping containers in the car. When used as tanks in the vacation quarters, they should be lined up out of the way of traffic and, as specimens are caught, compatible ones should be kept together. If personalities of various species are studied carefully, fishes will not have to be transferred from the time they have been caught until they reach their permanent quarters. An extra supply of jugs should be brought along for water containers but plastic bags can be used also for this purpose. One or two small jugs of two- to three-gallon capacity should be included for the storage of specimens while out in the boat. Plastic buckets can be used for this purpose also. All jugs should be equipped with sturdy handles.

An outboard motor is invaluable to the collector. It assures him of fairly rapid transportation from place to place and, in areas where weather is uncertain, it gives him assurance of getting in to shore quickly in the event of a sudden squall. Outboards are fairly expensive when rented and although skiffs are usually available in any area where fishing is popular, motors are often at a premium. Of course, the collector can operate without a boat, but only on a limited basis. The boat not only serves as a means of transportation but it is also useful in carrying equipment and serves as a headquarters on the water.

It has been our experience that keeping gear down to a minimum saves both energy and space. There are additional pieces of equipment, however, that to varying degrees are useful, if not essential. Swim flippers, glass-bottom buckets, snorkels (which we have already mentioned) and aqualungs fall into this category.

Glass-bottom buckets are helpful in finding likely spots and can be used both from the boat and while in the water. Using them from the boat saves going over the side so often. They can be purchased or put together rather easily by a do-it-yourself handyman. If you plan to make your own buckets, it is a good idea to size them so that one will fit into another in order to conserve space.

The aqualung adds more excitement to a vacation, as it can be used in deep water and enables the collector to explore the wonders of the submarine world. Most desirable specimens, however, can be found in water not more than four feet deep, which puts the aqualung in the luxury class in a collector's gear. It certainly broadens the scope and enriches the adventure of underwater swimming, however, and if the budget will allow it, we cannot think of any objection to adding it to one's equipment. But by all means take lessons in using it from a competent instructor before attempting to dive.

Swim flippers are fun to wear while swimming and reduce the amount of energy spent in getting from one place to another. When the collector is on his feet, however, which he often is, the flippers tend to stir up the bottom, clouding the water to the point where visibility is nil. If flippers are to be taken along, the collector should remember to buy them large enough to wear over sneakers.

The Hazards of Collecting

There are some dangerous aspects involved in collecting, some of which have been grossly exaggerated and others completely understated. It is well for the collector to be aware of all of them and to regard them in their proper perspective. Most accidents that occur in any pursuit are the result of carelessness or lack of knowledge of existing dangers.

Perhaps advice against overexposure to the sun will seem a bit unnecessary at this point. Nonetheless, many a vacation has been spoiled because the necessary precautions were not taken to avoid sunburn. Northerners are prone to be careless on this point and perhaps a warning will prevent what might have been a delightful vacation from being a painful ordeal. Florida sun is deceptive; a constant breeze from the sea prevents immediate discomfort and sometimes it isn't until the collector is back in his quarters that he discovers that the damage has been done. Fair-skinned people especially should be covered from neck to ankles while in a boat or on the beach working in tidepools. Many collectors go into the water fully clothed in shirt and trousers because they realize they will be constantly in and out of the water. A good silicon-based face lotion should be applied each morning to the neck and face before starting out. A tan should be acquired slowly. All of these suggestions are trite, no doubt, but a bad burn will keep the most ardent hobbyist incapacitated from a week to ten days.

Everyone has heard stories of predaceous fishes attacking swimmers and although many of these tales are apt to be embellished somewhat by the raconteur, there are too many reports of people being attacked by sharks, barracuda, or moray eels to ignore completely the possibility of such an occurrence. A human being, at best, is awkward in the water and his best defense against such attacks is not to invite them.

Do not allow legs to dangle over the side of a boat or raft. Remove all shiny objects from clothing or limbs before starting out in the water. Rings, bracelets, watches, etc. are better left behind. Never carry a dead, mutilated fish while wading in the water, and if scratched or cut, wait until the wound heals before going into the water. Never flail the water with legs or hands to create a splashing of water in play. If, while swimming under water, a barracuda is encountered, change your course without gestures of alarm. Usually the fish is merely curious and will keep its distance, unless it feels cornered. This could be the case if it were met by a collector swimming to his boat. If the fish found itself between the swimmer and the skiff, it might attack, feeling that it was being closed in. Give it plenty of time to make its departure before again trying to reach the boat.

Coral growths in shallow waters are often covered with coralines or other types of algae. These usually show up as green mounds in the water. It is better not to tread on such mounds as they may be the diurnal quarters of a moray eel. Although this eel is sluggish during the day, being a nighttime feeder, if stepped upon or kicked, it might retaliate by inflicting a painful wound on the trespasser.

Be careful of the place you put your feet down. If you suddenly decide to stop swimming and take a standing position, check the spot carefully for sea urchins before you place your feet on the bottom.

Spines from these marine animals puncture the skin and break off, causing a smarting sensation that can last quite a while. If this should happen, the spines should be removed as soon after the occurrence as possible. The punctures in the skin should be soaked with household ammonia or Clorox.

Abrasions in the skin caused by brushing against live coral should be treated in the same way to avoid infection. Avoid contacts with the tentacles of the man-o'-war jellyfish which is conspicuous by its inflated iridescent sac that floats atop the water. Long streamers hang from this animal and if they touch the body or hands, they leave whip-like welts on the flesh that are very painful.

Craig Phillips and Winfield H. Brady have written a little paper-bound book entitled *Sea Pests,* now unfortunately out of print. It is filled with information as to how to recognize poisonous marine life and also gives suggestions for treatment of injuries sustained through contact with such.

There are many safety rules in connection with using a boat, but perhaps one of the most important to remember is not to secure your boat by tying it to a stake or coral head. Lower your anchor any time you decide to leave your boat. It might move a little but it will not get away from you. Swimming after a boat that has come loose from its mooring has been the cause of many a tragic accident. Do not go out far when the weather is threatening. There is usually plenty of collecting territory within a hundred yards of the shore and a trip out to the reef can be postponed for a better day. Do not overcrowd a boat and do not venture out in one that is not equipped with lifesavers.

In the years that we have collected, we have never experienced a serious accident. Probably the worst that has happened to us is a brief encounter with a sea urchin. Using common sense and having some knowledge of the waters in which you are operating removes most of the danger connected with collecting.

The Art of Collecting

Collecting specimens is an art that develops with experience. Reef fishes are usually caught by the underwater method briefly described above. The collector either walks in the water approximately waist deep, and peers through his glass-bottom bucket for likely places for specimens on the ocean floor, or he swims face down wearing a face mask. When a sponge or coral bed is discovered, he studies it for a moment, watching for movement. Usually the first little fish he encounters is the beau gregory, a minute tyrant that patrols the area he has claimed as his own with an alertness and courage that would humble a Buckingham Palace guard. As he is apt to claim your aquarium and patrol it with the same zeal, he is better left to his vigilance on the ocean floor, even though his blue and yellow coloring is strikingly beautiful. When a suitable quarry is discovered, however, the collector manipulates a gloved hand and his net and, because these fishes seldom go far from home base, it isn't long before a capture is made.

Probably the most difficult part of this type of collecting is the skill of learning to spot specimens. Lighting effects under water are tricky and, although it would seem that the vivid colors displayed by the reef fishes would make them conspicuous, they often serve as a perfect camouflage. After some experience, however, the collector's eye becomes trained to catch movement and color.

Careful handling after specimens have been caught is most important. The fish should be placed in the bucket or jug in the boat immediately after its capture. In one article, written by a professional collector, it was suggested that a long, stocking-type net be used so that each fish could be tied off as it was caught to save the collector the time of returning to the boat. Such a method might save time, but the condition of the specimens after having been dragged through the water would be such that it is doubtful whether they would survive the trip home from the boat, not to mention lasting through shipment or transfer by automobile to their final destination. The storage container should be covered by a straw hat or some other light object for protection from the sun. If the time spent out in the water runs into hours, the water in the storage container should be partially changed from time to time.

Do not take fishes that are seen swimming in schools among the coral heads and sponges. These fishes are travelers and although they are colorful, they do not adapt well to aquarium life. Such schools are usually made up of grunts, schoolmasters, parrot fish and porkfish. Their behavior pattern is so different from that of the reef fishes that after a few moments of study the collector can distinguish them easily. The reef specimens, such as the French, black, queen, and blue angels are never seen in schools when they are youngsters. The butter-fly fishes, too, are usually found living singly, or in pairs, in a territory they have chosen as a kind of home or headquarters. A careful reading of the characteristics of the desirable aquarium fishes will help the aquarist to discriminate between those fishes that adjust well to aquarium life and those that do not.

Large specimens, of course, should be left behind for reasons we have explained in previous chapters. Leaving such specimens is not only wise from the aquarist's point of view, but it is also a means of conservation.

Catching floating masses of sargassum weed in a net is another method of collecting. This can be done while wading or from a slowly moving boat. The net is thrust under the seaweed and lifted. The net should then be allowed to settle in the water or in a partially filled bucket of water in the boat. Each piece of the plant is rinsed before it is removed from the net and thrown back into the water. When the net is free of all the seaweed, it is examined for the little hitch-hikers that ride in the sargassum weed without any particular destination in view. Occasionally a filefish will be discovered or a sargassum fish. Both these fishes should be studied for personality traits before they are considered as aquarium specimens. Trunkfish have been collected in this manner, and the young of certain game fish.

Seines are used when collecting along the shore or over the grass flats. Slow-moving fishes such as sea horses, baby cowfish, spiny box-fish, etc. are collected in this manner. The seine should be equipped on either end with a wooden rod similar to a broom handle. Two collectors, one on either end of the seine, with handles held so that the lower part of the seine is dragged evenly over the ocean floor, walk slowly along. When the seine is loaded with material, it is lifted so that it hangs like a hammock between the collectors. The material is then examined for likely specimens. This method is especially good for estuaries and inlets of northern waters.

Traps and dragnets can also be employed for collecting specimens. The use of traps is a rather long, drawn-out process and unless the collector is planning to spend considerable time at the collecting site, it is better to depend on more reliable methods. The dragnet can be towed from a boat. The net should be constructed of wire mesh with substantial frame and bridled so that the lower side of the frame scrapes along the ocean floor. When the net becomes heavy with material it can be lifted and its contents examined. This is a hit-or-miss method at best, and the system of employing a seine is more satisfactory.

As soon as specimens are established in aerated five-gallon jugs at the vacation headquarters, a feeding routine should be started. Brine-shrimp eggs should be in the process of hatching the day of arrival. A dry food prepared especially for marine tropicals should be at hand to begin the adjustment to aquarium fare. Salt-water fishes seem to recover very rapidly from the shock of being caught and within a few hours after their capture, they are usually willing to accept food. The new specimens should receive all the care recently purchased fishes are tendered (*see* Chapter 3).

Conservation

When collecting was relatively new, the subject of conservation was often dismissed by collectors as being purely academic. Within a seven-year period, however, the value of conservation has been poignantly brought home to us by finding places, which only a few years ago were rich with marine life, now in a state of desolation.

As we have explained before, reef fishes usually select a sponge or coral head for a home. Sometimes they take up living quarters in a sunken barrel or even under a board that is waterlogged and lies on the ocean floor. The very arrangement of the area the fish has chosen for its home may mean life or death to it and countless other tiny creatures. Such a spot should be left exactly as it was found. If the board was placed so that it covered a hollow, try to leave it in its original position.

There is no reason to rip up sponges and break them needlessly, nor should a barrel be disturbed to the point that it is not accessible to the countless living things that have depended on it as a refuge in an area where predators abound.

We have found places where the sponges had been large and

healthy, affording many small compartments for colorful little tenants, bare and empty except for the broken fingers of sponges that were half buried in the marl. The brightly colored creatures that had once given the spot life had long since disappeared.

The natives of the Florida Keys are growing resentful of hobbyists who take home a collection of fishes at the cost of leaving such scenes of desolation behind them. Many of us are still respected there, but unless collectors set up a code of conservation among themselves, it won't be many years before they will be unwelcome to such interesting places as the Florida Keys.

Set up your own conservation program and take only the number of fishes that your tanks can support. If your number of aquariums is limited, keep in mind that although collecting conditions may be excellent, you cannot afford to take home more than four or five specimens to a tank. As large specimens do not adjust well to aquarium life, they are best left behind. We have collected with a public exhibitor of marine life who shunned large specimens not only with the adaptibility of the fishes in mind but with the thought that unless large specimens are left to breed, the reef population will eventually diminish.

It isn't the number of fishes taken that makes a collecting expedition successful. To find two black or French angels living in harmony in one spot is a far better catch than six of the same varieties of fishes caught in various places who will undoubtedly fight each other to the death if confined to one aquarium. Even the remaining victor will probably be so bruised as a result of its conquests that it will become the host of parasites of one kind or another to which it will finally succumb.

If we collectors form and practice our own conservation rules, the governments of the states involved will not have to do it for us.

Collecting Coral, Shells and Sand

The coral found along the shores of the Florida Keys is considerably different in structure and texture than that which dealers usually display in their showcases. Although most of the coral offered for sale has been taken from the waters off the Florida Keys, occasionally it is imported from Australia and India. Whatever the source, the coral sold in aquarium stores and gift shops is usually beautifully formed pieces of staghorn, or symmetrical heads of brain coral or other types that take on characteristic forms. It comes from the great reefs made up of many different species of coral that form natural barriers in the sea and are collected by professionals with craft equipped with the necessary diving and blasting gear.

What we know to be coral is actually the calcareous skeleton or remains of one of the coelenterates, a tiny anemone-like marine animal that secretes calcium from its outer skin, forming a hard, protective cup around itself. It reproduces through budding, the term for its progenitive process which is the development of a complete new organism from a protuberance that forms on its body. As the budding goes on, new individuals form and build on the calcareous remains of their ancestors, and what is called a colony takes shape. The conformation of colonies varies, depending on the species which compose them.

Unless the aquarist has access to the necessary equipment for collecting corals on the outer reefs, he contents himself with the type that is found high and dry on the shore. The live corals found in shallow waters should be shunned, for aquarium use, as they do not survive in captivity and, in the process of dying, give off gases and waste materials which pollute the water.

The best type of coral for aquarium use is that which is actually the foundation of part of the Florida Keys. It is made up of the calcium deposits of perhaps eight different marine animals along with sand, shells and calcareous algae all cemented together. Once exposed to the hot tropical sun and air, this mixture hardens and is referred to as dead coral rock. Sometimes pieces of this material are found in the intertidal zones where various boring mollusks drill holes in them in which they live. They pave the way for other creatures, some of which are not equipped to tunnel into a rocklike substance but are perfectly willing to move into such quarters when they are available. Because these pieces of coral have been perforated, they are often more interesting than those found along roadsides or near excavations. Unfortunately, they are not safe to use, for the mollusks who have paved the way for smaller creatures have also allowed them to become infested with minute crustacea that penetrate and break down the interiors until they become soft and vermiculated. Such coral, even if boiled, would contain so much organic material that it would be a source of pollution in the aquarium.

Pieces of dead coral rock are also found away from the intertidal zone. Sometimes they are piled in heaps by excavations or they are strewn along a highway. Coral found in such locations is generally solid although occasionally some will have holes. The solid pieces can be modified, however, for aquarium use. Holes can be made in them with a hammer and chisel (or tire iron), and existing holes can be made larger and deeper with the same tools. Coral that is stained with

Robson Nelson

Figure 17.

Dead coral rock in background. Algae is growing profusely on rear wall of this aquarium. French or black angel (*Pomacanthus paru*) Bloch, or *Pomacanthus arcuatus*, Linnaeus) and four-eyed butterfly (*Chaetodon capistratus*, Linnaeus) are in the foreground.

oil or tar should not be taken. While collecting pieces of coral rock along roadsides and in fields, the hands and feet should be well protected. Scorpions and other such unfriendly creatures capable of inflicting stings and bites often lurk in such unmolested places as coral piles in open fields and by deserted roadsides. Before any of the collected pieces are used in the aquarium they should be boiled for twenty minutes in a clean enamel pan and baked in an oven at a low temperature (*see* Figures 17 and 60).

Coral that has been taken from the intertidal zone because of interesting formation might be kept outdoors in a sunny place, away from where it might be sprayed with insecticide, weedkillers or soluble fertilizers. Eventually, after months of baking in the sun, it will harden throughout. When it produces a ringing sound when tapped with a solid object it may be used in the aquarium. The ringing tone indicates that it has hardened to its core.

Shells can be used in the aquarium as decorative pieces and should be chosen large enough so that they may serve as hiding places for specimens. The spires or cones of the shells should be cut away so that they will not become pockets where decaying debris can collect. Conch shells (*see* Figure 60) make excellent hideaways for fishes as well as contributing to the beauty of the aquarium. Whelks, channeled and knobbed, are found along the beaches up and down the east and west coasts and their shells, when the spires are cut away, make interesting as well as useful aquarium pieces.

All shells should be thoroughly cleaned before they are placed in the tank. If any tissue is left from the animals that once occupied them, it should be completely scraped away. The boiling and oven-heating process recommended for coral may be used for shells also. Sun-baking in the open is another method if the shells give off an odor or cannot otherwise be freed of tissue. Never use acids or other chemicals for cleaning either shells or coral.

The skeletons of gorgonians, or sea whips, calcareous algae, make good hitching posts for sea horses. They are found washed up on shore occasionally. Sometimes they are referred to by aquarists as "deadman's fingers." These should be thoroughly dried by the sun. When ready for aquarium use, they should not give off any odor. The calcified holdfast makes a fine base which when caught between two pieces of

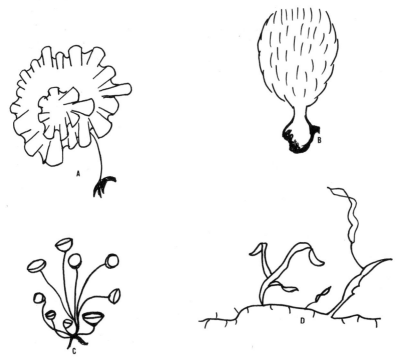

Figure 18. MARINE PLANTS THAT HAVE BEEN KEPT IN SALT-WATER AQUARIUMS

A Sea lettuce (ulva). This is a common green alga, found along most seashores of the United States. It has been successfully maintained in aquariums where both aeration and sunlight are present. It is a delicacy to a number of fishes, however, and for this reason doesn't remain long enough to become established where these particular species are included in the aquarium community. **B** Merman's shaving brush (*Penicillus capitatus*); **C** Mermaid's cup (*Acetabularia*); **D** Caulerpa.

All of these plants might be subjects of experiments in tanks that do not include fishes. The mermaid's cup is as delicately beautiful as its name suggests, and all four of these algae are green. Deterioration, however, of sea algae is a rapid process; if salt water is scarce, it is advisable not to risk it through pollution which may very well occur when experimenting with algae, if fishes are of prime interest.

coral in the aquarium, holds the skeleton at the desired angle. Sea horses like to curl their tails around the ends of the fingers and lunge after brine shrimps as they move by.

Rocks of any type, unless the aquarist can be sure of his ability to identify them, should be left behind. Traces of metals may be in them that would oxidize in salt water. Limestone can be used but if identification is hazy, it should be rejected.

A few handfuls of fine beach sand should be taken to mix with the coral and shell sand found on the southeastern coast of Florida. If the aquarist doesn't have access to the coral and shell sand, he should use quartz that he has purchased from his dealer. In any case, only enough barely to cover the bottom of the aquarium should be used. The few handfuls of beach sand is recommended because it is beneficial to some marine animals. Sand should be boiled and dried before being used in the aquarium.

The types of sand peculiar to various coastal regions are painstakingly described in Rachel Carson's *The Edge of the Sea,* a work which has been mentioned previously as a wealth of information for the aquarist who collects his specimens.

If the aquarist wants to try his luck at keeping plants, it is suggested that he take those that grow in the shade of bridges or rocks. These will have a better chance for survival than those that have been pampered by constant sunshine. The algae selected should be carefully handled and will do much better if transferred in an aerated container. It is not suggested, however, that they be placed in jugs that contain specimens. See Figure 18 for the names and identification of the algae that do best in aquariums. Experimenting with algae should be carried on in aquariums set aside for this purpose only.

Collecting Crabs, Anemones and Shrimp

Hermit crabs, one species or another, are found almost everywhere within sound of the sea. There are some that have moved permanently out of the water but are always found within its proximity. There are others that scurry back and forth from the sea to the land, and back to the sea again, running countless errands of importance only to hermit crabs. The intertidal zone is their territory and although they have left their mother, the great ocean, they have done so only on a part-time basis. There are still others who are entirely tied to their mother's apron strings and never leave the water. They are found scuttling across the ocean floor, sometimes miles from the shoreline, with no apparent inclination to explore the rocks and crannies that have lured the more precocious members of their family to new ways of life.

The land crabs have adapted to life on the shore and obviously have no place in the aquarium. The part-time ocean dweller has no place in it either for when so confined it becomes frustrated because of its inability to fulfill its destiny. It paces the tank floor constantly because its liaison with the land is interrupted and in its fruitless effort to escape, it becomes a disturbing factor to the other members of the aquarium community.

To avoid taking species of hermit crabs that are unsuited to aquarium life, collect your specimens some distance from the shore. The striped hermit crab (*Clibanarious vittatus*) makes a very fine aquarium pet (*see* Figures 5 and 6). This species is found along the southern Atlantic coast, and, along with many other species of hermit crabs discovered in all the coastal waters of the United States, has made no commitments that bring it to the land and will be content to spend its time policing your aquarium floor for tidbits.

Do not take too many hermit crabs but plan to have two for each aquarium with a capacity over forty gallons and one each for those having less. We have taken hermits that were about the size of a pea but perhaps those the size of marbles would be more effective. They grow fairly rapidly but it takes well over a year before they become objectionably large. By the time they reach ping-pong-ball dimensions, they have become pets and their release back into the sea has its ceremonial aspects.

Be sure that you have a collection of shells graduated in size, for these little fellows become very unhappy if forced to remain in shells they have outgrown. (See Chapter 2 for their feeding and other requirements.)

They may be taken home in a jug that contains fishes but should not be put into an already crowded container. Hermit crabs give off considerable amounts of urea and, of course, require oxygen. One to a five-gallon jug containing three fishes not more than two inches long might be a practical rule; or, five hermit crabs to a five-gallon jug with no fishes present.

Hermit crabs that vary considerably in size should never be kept together. Larger ones feel no compuctions about forcibly evicting smaller ones from shells that are of no interest to them whatever. When two are placed in an aquarium, care must be taken that they compare favorably in size for any appreciable variance sparks a contest in which the niceties of rules are unknown.

Although hermit crabs at best are drab little creatures parading around in borrowed finery, and are completely devoid of any of the finer feelings for one another, they frequently win the affection of their owners. This is due in part, no doubt, to the comical picture they present when scrambling clumsily for a tidbit or when tenderly measuring with outstretched antennae the interior of a prospective home. They are far too slow to harm a healthy fish and because they are ever vigilant in policing the aquarium floor for any scraps of food overlooked by the fishes, they earn their place in the aquarium community.

Sea anemones are found in the coastal waters of the United States in both drab and dramatic forms. Some resemble large flowers in both form and color while others are but small brown or pale green plume-like growths.

The *Condylactus passiflora* (*see* Figure 7), which are by far the most beautiful of the anemones of Atlantic waters, are found in colonies in rather shallow water along the shores of mangrove islands of the Florida Keys. We have taken them from both the Gulf and Atlantic sides. Sometimes they are white with scarlet-tipped tentacles. Often they are tinted in delicate shades of pink or orchid. Always they are lovely to see and the aquarist may be tempted to take more than he can support. One of these flowerlike animals is enough for any aquarium and there are hobbyists who shun them entirely, believing their waste products are detrimental to the other members of the aquarium. In our experience, however, we have found no evidence to substantiate this belief. Small specimens are more desirable than large unless the aquarist is prepared to keep them in a tank to themselves. Incidentally, size does not determine the age of an anemone; rather, it indicates the quality of conditions in which the animal has lived. It is not important that the aquarist determine the age of the specimen he is considering for his aquarium as anemones are extremely long-lived. Size is the test as to whether the specimen in question is desirable or not. The small specimens, measuring approximately two to three inches across, give off less waste material and require less food than large specimens and generally do better in captivity.

Many interesting anemones are found in northern waters, and although these are not so dramatic as the *Condylactus passiflora* of the Florida Keys, they are often delicately tinted and add interest to the aquarium.

Anemones should be removed carefully from the lump of coral or other surface to which they are attached. They can be handled with the fingers but usually a sharp knife is needed to remove them without damage. If the anchorage is a small stone or a bit of coral, take it along with the specimen. Once in a jug, the anemone will probably move away from it of its own volition and the stone or piece of coral can be discarded. Anemones heal rather quickly when injured, but as some wounds are fatal to them, care in handling is most advisable. They may be transferred in aerated jugs and only one small specimen should be included in a five-gallon jug containing two fishes measuring less than two inches long. If the aquarist has collected several, a five-gallon aerated jug should be used without fishes present.

Spider crabs (*Stenorynchus seticornis*), coral shrimps (*Stenopus hispidus*), mantis shrimps (*Squilla empusa*) and ghost shrimps (*Callianassa Stimpsoni*) are all interesting and innocuous in the aquarium. Spider crabs are often found in the sea grasses and coral shrimps are discovered in coral beds or near urchin colonies. Both of these marine animals are found in waters off the Florida Keys. The mantis shrimps and ghost shrimps are found in northern waters and are often scooped up in nets that have been thrust under clumps of seaweed.

The spider crab is most grotesquely attractive and the banded coral shrimp not only adds color to the aquarium but delights the aquarist with its regal mannerisms. We have not been successful in keeping the coral shrimp for any length of time and have concluded that diet seems to be part of the problem. We believe a tank containing coral that is well covered with a growth of algae may very well be the solution. It just so happened that on the two different occasions we acquired specimens of the coral shrimp, our tanks were newly set up and no algae were present.

The mantis shrimp and ghost shrimp do well enough in captivity despite the fact that the aquarium does not afford them the pleasure of burrowing which both of them enjoy in natural surroundings. Ghost shrimps thrive especially well in the aquarium and these transparent creatures always draw exclamations of surprise from their audience when they suddenly swim out from under a piece of coral.

Summary

We have not attempted to list all the interesting animals that the aquarist may find while collecting in the various coastal areas. Such a catalog would be a book in itself. Some of the most interesting marine specimens are mentioned in the books listed as suggested reading at the end of this chapter. Certainly any one of these works is invaluable to the collector as a means of identifying the various creatures encountered in littoral waters.

For the most part, we have merely tried to establish the groundwork for a successful collecting expedition, posting warnings here and there where we think they are necessary, and suggesting methods and equipment to save time, energy and unnecessary expense.

We have mentioned the Florida Keys many times with reference to collecting because the waters there are rich in the multicolored reef fishes which have become favorites among aquarists universally. The areas in the world where brightly hued marine animals, such as the reef fishes, may be found are not common and we are particularly fortunate to have such an area included in the coastline of our country.

The interesting specimens collected, however, do not have to be reef fishes alone. There are many species of fishes highly prized among aquarists that are found in waters off both the east and west coasts of the United States.

Certain pipefishes are found in waters off Maine and sea horses are collected as far north as Cape Cod. One sea horse is found in southern Californian waters—the giant sea horse (*Hippocampus ingens*).

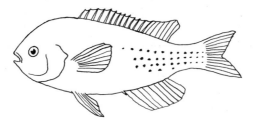

Figure 19. BLACKSMITH (*Ayresia punctipinnis,* Cooper)

Bays and estuaries up and down the northeastern seaboard are extremely fine collecting grounds. Present are not only such northern fishes as the sticklebacks and killifishes, but occasionally visitors from the tropics are picked up there, such as the butterfly fishes, spiny box-fishes, and members of the Monacanthidae family, the filefishes. The trunkfishes, too, are sometimes swept northward by the currents that move away from the equator.

Waters off southern California have no reef fishes comparable to those indigenous to the Florida coast, but there are many interesting species found there. The kelp beds and tidepools are favorite collecting spots. Of the family Pomacentridae of which the Beau Gregory and sergeant major of Florida waters are members, only two species are represented: *Ayresia punctipinnis* (Cooper), the blacksmith; and *Hypsypops rubincundus* (Girard), the garibaldi (*see* Figures 19 and 20). The blacksmith is slate-black, tinged with blue; some scales are edged in green. The fins are blue-black and the soft dorsal and caudal are

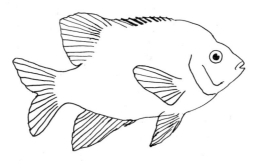

Figure 20. GARIBALDI (*Hypsypops rubicundus,* Girard)

profusely spotted. The garibaldi is bright blue when about an inch long and later becomes an orange-red. Although this is a spectacular species, it has not been included in our chapters on fishes because it is pugnacious and has not been generally available to aquarists. Both of these fishes, although related to species thought of as salt-water tropicals, are not particularly favored by aquarists. There are many fishes, however, found in the coastal waters of California that are generally accepted by hobbyists. Pipefishes, killifishes, spadefishes, sticklebacks, are among the specimens found there. (Figure 21 shows spadefish.)

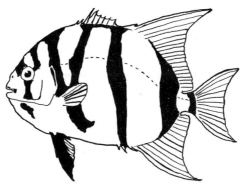

Figure 21. PACIFIC SPADEFISH (*Chaetodipterus zonatus,* Girard)

The actual haunts of desirable aquarium specimens have been barely touched upon in our chapter on collecting, as specific advice of this nature would be misleading at best. All specimens on occasion show up where one least expects them and areas that appear tailored for a particular fish are often disappointing. Some of the most beautiful of the reef fishes are found in waters within a mile of the shoreline of the Florida Keys. The ones best suited to aquarium life are those that stay close to their respective home bases. The wanderers, such as the grunts and parrot fishes, although extremely colorful, do not adjust to aquarium life and are best left behind. The comparatively slow-moving fishes, such as sea horses and pipefishes, are discovered in the grass flats which abound on both sides of the Keys. Grass flats of other coastal areas are usually rich with marine fauna also. Floating masses of sargassum weed often contain specimens interesting to collectors.

Tidepools and sea caves are treasure grounds for collectors. These are all broad generalities, though, with which experienced collectors are familiar. In developing his own knowledge as to where particular specimens are found, the amateur collector comes upon the most exciting aspect of his hobby, the thrill of personal discovery. His skill as a collector grows from such experience and the trend his hobby takes becomes a form of self-expression.

In previous chapters we have warned the aquarist against including such specimens as sea urchins, sea slugs, sea cucumbers and starfish with aquarium fishes. These invertebrates do, however, have a certain fascination and there is no reason why tanks for them alone cannot be maintained. We have posted warnings when we thought the well-being of fishes was at stake; we have no wish to inhibit the aquarist to the point of not making discoveries for himself.

The game fisherman is not alone in his propensity for spinning yarns. The amateur collector has a wistful repertoire of his own about "the one that got away." We eat at a little restaurant called the Coral Grill in Islamorada. The proprietor is a large, solemn-faced gentleman named Ed, concerned mainly with the mundane business of feeding hungry and sometimes impatient fishermen. His wife, Tess, does the cooking and only once in a while can she take time out to give us a friendly greeting during the busy mealtimes. Between orders for ham and eggs, or coffee black, however, Ed finds time to come over to our table, and with his grave blue eyes looking seaward, he'll say: "It's going to be good today." We grin at one another and feel a pleasure in knowing that he shares our adventure with us. In the evening, long after the hungry crowd has been fed and has dispersed, we go down to the grill and relate to Ed and Tess the surprises of the day. The ocean has been our grab bag and although Ed and Tess will not, until their retirement, share its treasures with us, they want to hear, over cups of hot black coffee, about the brave little Beau Gregory, all of two inches long, who tried to drive us away from his castle under the sea, a rusty beer can; or the ray who was as big as a grand piano and found reason to jump high out of the sea and make a very temporary blot against the blue sky. We bask in the attention of a receptive audience and are impatient for the night to pass so that we can return to the gardens under the sea.

Suggested Reading

Percy Spencer Barnhart, *Marine Fishes of Southern California,* University of California Press.

N. J. Berrill, *The Living Tide,* Fawcett Publications (paperback edition).

*Charles M. Breder, Jr., *Field Book of Marine Fishes of the Atlantic Coast,* G. P. Putnam's Sons.

Rachel Carson, *The Edge of the Sea,* Houghton Mifflin Company.

*Roy Waldo Miner, *Field Book of Seashore Life,* G. P. Putnam's Sons (covers North Atlantic coast only).

*Herbert S. Zim and Lester Ingle, *Seashores,* Simon and Schuster (a Golden Nature Guide).

*Herbert S. Zim and Hurst H. Shoemaker, *Fishes—A Guide to Familiar American Species* (a Golden Nature Guide).

---

*Books recommended to be used in the field as references for identification.

PART TWO

DATA ON SALT-WATER AQUARIUM FISHES

CHAPTER 6

General Considerations

THE NOTES on the various species given in this section of our book
have been gleaned from sources we deem reliable. Many of them
stem directly from our own experience in the hobby. The fishes mentioned are, for the most part, those that have become popular among
aquarists during the last several years and are, of course, species that
have been available. Many of the fishes chosen have been selected
solely because they have been studied for substantial periods and information has been developed as to their particular requirements
and personalities. Some species have been noted that are not completely satisfactory aquarium fishes, simply because they do appear
on dealers' lists and their colorful descriptions might tempt the aquarist to acquire them without first considering their adaptability to the
home aquarium.

We have not attempted to catalog all the likely candidates among
the marine tropicals for the home aquarium. At this time such a list
cannot be compiled, as there are many specimens that have never
been introduced into this country that might well fall into this category. They are slated to be the highlights of future editions of this
book. Even now there are species coming into the country that are
spectacular and may be in many cases completely adaptable to the
home aquarium but they have not been available long enough for
fair appraisal.

Our principal aim in writing our book is to aid aquarists in maintaining healthy salt-water fishes for satisfactory lengths of time. Because species differ somewhat in requirements and in personality traits,
we feel that the various popular salt-water fishes should be discussed
individually. In our treatment of each fish, we have included a description, located it geographically, listed its idiosyncracies, its food
preferences, and appraised it generally for home aquarium adaptability.

We have not gone into scale counts or other technical data relative to scientific classification because such information is seldom of interest to the aquarist. For those who seek it, however, many worthy volumes (some of which are cited throughout this book) have been written on this subject. If they are not on the shelves of the average bookstore, they can be obtained from many of the larger public libraries.

We have divided the popular salt-water aquarium fishes into three categories: Marine Aquarium Fishes from Atlantic Waters; The Exotics; and The Estuary Fishes. The chapter devoted to the exotics deals with marine fishes not indigenous to the United States that have been imported.

Many of the exotic marine tropicals have proved to be highly successful aquarium fishes. Impressive longevity records are available on them which often outshine the reports that have come to our attention on fishes from our own native waters. This may be the result of the expert handling the exotics received when collected and during the period they were kept before shipment to this country; or it may be due to the fact that their requirements are not so exacting as those of the marine tropicals indigenous to our coastal waters. We are inclined to believe, however, that with proper handling, our native tropicals will do as well in the home aquarium as the exotics. We have found from our own experiments that if water conditions are poor, neither the natives nor the exotics survive, and they are both equally susceptible to parasitic infection. Tolerance to conditions does vary among salt-water fishes, however, regardless of source, and these will be discussed in the sections that follow on individual species.

It has been noted by many writers of works on marine life that in tropical waters where temperatures are constant, where the abundance of food is more or less the same all year round, and where coral reefs abound, many species of fishes are present. Coral thrives only in water that seldom becomes colder than 70° Fahrenheit and such constant temperatures are limited to areas where currents of warm water travel away from the equator toward the poles, within the Tropic of Cancer and the Tropic of Capricorn. Currents traveling toward the poles are prevalent on eastern coasts of continents. Currents on western coasts of continents move toward the equator, and even in the tropical belt the sea is cold. The great coral reefs of the world, therefore, are found off the eastern coasts of continents, providing hiding places and food for many forms of marine life. Such an ideal environment becomes a natural pilot plant for the mutations—variances within a species—occurring there, offering them a better chance for survival than would be available in waters subject to climatic change where living calls for sturdiness and endurance. Tropical waters where coral reefs flourish, therefore, become a kind of natural marine biological laboratory where nature's new models receive their initial tests for survival. Here many variances within a species succeed or fail in an ecology that is for the most part favorable compared with other parts of the ocean. Because of the static conditions, however, the many species that survive here are kept at rather constant numbers in populations. So, on the one hand, while mutations might very well become established here, because living is uncomplicated by changing conditions, the possibility of the numbers of individuals within a species increasing dramatically is checked by the stability of the food supply. Therefore we find many kinds of fishes in tropical waters, some bizarre in shape, and others striking in color, but the numbers of individuals within a species are few compared with those found in northern waters where great schools of fishes follow the ever-shifting grazing fields of plankton. Here we have no laboratory with controlled conditions; instead, we have great variances in temperature and food supplies and only the species survive that can take the ever-changing conditions. The number of species thins out the farther north we go, but because plankton thrives where changes of temperature cause upwelling or vertical currents, the populations of the various kinds of species that do survive in northern waters are vast and fluctuate with the amounts of plankton available. These fishes can meet the task of swimming long distances to feeding grounds and they can endure the wide differences in temperature they encounter.

We have outlined these observations on marine animals of northern and southern waters because they have a significance to the aquarist. The northern fishes, for the most part, do not lend themselves to the aquarium from any standpoint. They are wanderers, which makes them unsuitable for confinement and they are conservative in shape and color, which makes them uninteresting to the hobbyist who looks for the strange and unusual. On the other hand, among the many species of fishes found in the tropical seas, there are some that do little or no traveling at all. Confinement in an aquarium is not a hardship for them and they need and expect the controlled conditions the aquarist can offer. Because they are not conservative in either shape or color, they are extremely interesting to the hobbyist and in almost all respects these fishes lend themselves to what is proving to be a most fascinating hobby. As the salt-water tropicals are more or less pampered in their natural environment by constant conditions, the aquarist, in order to keep them successfully, must strive to match the ecology these fishes have found in nature. The limited area in which they live is indicative of the narrow margin of variance which they can endure, and the constancy of chemical environment, temperature and nutrition to which they are accustomed must be duplicated by the aquarist as closely as possible.

For the hobbyist who does not choose to expend this kind of effort and yet finds salt-water fishes worthy of attention, there are the fishes found in both native and foreign estuaries. These species are perhaps the most tolerant of the salt-water varieties. They have succeeded in living in waters that are often contaminated by human and industrial waste products. They do not wander far because the food on which they thrive is abundant and constant in their environment which, however, is often not constant in either temperature or chemical make-up. Many of them can live in brackish water and some can be converted to fresh water entirely. Although these fishes do not match the coral fishes in color, they are often interesting in design and many of them have intriguing personalities. Certainly they are worthy of consideration and mention.

Temperaments of various fishes differ and often catastrophe results if this phase of the hobby is not carefully considered. There are many combinations of fishes that do live harmoniously together, and these will be treated in our summary for the second part of our book.

Prices of fishes often baffle the most experienced marine aquarist. Sometimes specimens that have been shipped halfway around the world are priced lower than those shipped from relatively short distances. When the aquarist does his own collecting, he learns which varieties are seldom seen or are more difficult to catch than others. It comes as a surprise to him to discover that quite often the most elusive of the fishes he has collected are priced below those that are comparatively easier to find and catch. This may be due to the fact that the professional collector has come upon an easy system of catching the particular fish the aquarist found difficult to capture, or he may have discovered a spot where these individuals are plentiful. Whatever the reasons that lie behind prices quoted by dealers, we are sure that as the hobby grows, the cost of specimens will drop considerably. This has already happened in a number of instances in the period that salt-water specimens have become available, and as knowledge and know-how circulate among dealers and aquarists, much of the financial risk of handling marine fishes will be eliminated, which should affect prices favorably from the aquarists' point of view. This, coupled with a rising demand, will do much to place the hobby in a price bracket that most of us can afford.

CHAPTER 7

Marine Aquarium Fishes from Atlantic Waters

French and Black Angelfishes

THE young of the French angel (*Pomacanthus paru,* Bloch) and the black angel (*Pomacanthus arcuatus,* Linnaeus) look so much alike that only a scale and dorsal spine count can identify them, despite the many formulas for identification that have been presented in books written for marine aquarists. The prospective purchaser of specimens measuring from an inch to three inches from nose to tail will do well to choose the one that can be bought for the lowest price for if his dealer has priced one higher than the other, he has only been guessing which of his collection are black angels and which are French.

Actually, if identification could be determined, the French angel might be preferred over the black by the aquarist if only for the reason that in the adult stage the former attains a length of something over a foot, while the adult black angel is said to measure twenty-four inches from head to tail. But as few aquarists could accommodate either fish in the adult stage and since the young of both

Helen Simkatis

Figure 22.

This is a French or black angelfish (*Pomacanthus paru*, Bloch, or *Pomacanthus arcuatus*, Linnaeus).

varieties look exactly alike, there is little reason to worry whether the specimen in question is a French or black angel.

When these fishes reach adulthood, distinguishing them is no problem. The black angel shows no yellow on the body and although the inner sides of the pectoral fins are yellow, they are not seen when folded against the body. The adult French angel has gun-metal to brown scales edged with yellow and at the base of each pectoral fin is a bright yellow to orange stripe.

The French or black angelfish juvenile is among the most striking of the salt-water tropicals. It is a compressed, deep fish with velvet black as a basic body color which is broken by three yellow vertical stripes. Another vertical yellow stripe appears in the center of the caudal fin. There are yellow markings about the head which add interest and the long ventral fins are black, shot with bright blue along the posterior edges. This blue apears on the edge of the anal fin, too, but all traces of blue are lost as the specimen takes on size. The yellow stripes also disappear gradually as the fish matures, but this is a long process. A specimen we had for eighteen months grew from dime size to about four and a half inches long from head to tail, and in that time the rear stripe on the body had just begun to fade.

Both the French and black angels are found in waters off the Florida Keys and the West Indies. The young are usually discovered alone near a coral bed or clumps of marine plants where hiding places are available. They seldom travel far from what has been chosen as a base and leave it only when it has been disturbed and pillaged by thoughtless collectors.

These angels adjust very well to aquarium conditions. They will not usually attack other fishes but they will inflict injury on another of their own kind. One of two black or French angels becomes the aggressor and the other its victim. This is true no matter how small the specimens may be or how they vary in size. In a tank where several are present, one becomes the bully over the others and if it is removed, another steps up from the ranks to take its place; the death of its victims eventually ensues. A specimen measuring from three to four inches from snout to tail will hunt a dime-sized youngster down until it kills it and there is no successful formula in varying the sizes. Once in a great while, two specimens are found that tolerate one another, but this is so rare that it merely accents the general rule. The only method one can use to ascertain whether or not two are compatible is to watch them either in their natural surroundings or in a dealer's tank for at least a half hour. If, after studying the two in question under normal conditions no skirmish occurs, it may be safe to take them home to one aquarium. It may be that such a pair are male and female but this is pure conjecture, as sex is impossible to establish. Only a post-mortem examination will reveal the sex of these fishes and we have never followed through on this when we have lost two that were on friendly terms.

The aquarist may be reasonably certain, however, when he selects a specimen of either a French or black angelfish that it will not attack other kinds of fishes. We have heard of instances where this was not true, but in our experience with them we have never had one that bullied a fish of another species.

These angelfishes are not only strikingly beautiful but, as fishes go, they are extremely intelligent. Within a day of capture, a specimen usually accepts food from the fingers and very soon learns to recognize the person who feeds it.

Lettuce must be included in the diet of these fishes if algae are not present on the walls of the aquarium. The lettuce should be supplied in tiny pieces as the fish is unable to take large pieces because of its small mouth. Lettuce is a substitute for an important part of the fish's diet, but it is a strange food. It should therefore be introduced in such a way that it will be accepted. It is a good idea to start the feeding with lettuce. The first offering may be refused but if nothing more is given at the time, it will eventually be accepted. After several pieces have been taken and eaten, the aquarist may go on with the feeding, which should consist of tiny pieces of raw shrimp, or beef. These pieces should be small enough so that the fish can take them into its mouth without gaping. Brine shrimp should be offered several times a day if the specimen measures only a little over an inch from head to tail. Such a fish is barely out of the post-larval stage and aquarists who have dealt with fresh-water fishes know how often the very small fry should be fed. As the specimen takes on size, the number of feedings can be gradually cut down, but they should then be increased in bulk.

As mentioned before, it is said that adult black angels sometimes attain the length of twenty-four inches from head to tail but how old such a specimen is when it is this large is not known. The rate of growth can be indicated by the following example. A thumbnail-sized specimen was placed in a thirty-five gallon tank with one other fish, a butterfly (*Chaetodon capistratus*). In eighteen months the angelfish measured about four and a half inches from nose to tail. This would suggest that a thirty-five- or fifty-gallon tank would accommodate a French or black angelfish with several other fishes present for at least three years.

French and black angels are highly susceptible to toxic conditions. When water in an aquarium becomes chemically unbalanced, they are usually the first specimens to show distress. The black portions of the body become spotty and the breathing becomes rapid. Normally, the respiration rate is about seventy-two times a minute. If the breathing becomes considerably faster than this when the fish has not been highly active or has not been recently fed, and the body shows discoloration, some type of toxicity might be suspected.

One of our first reasonably successful ventures with salt-water specimens involved the use of a tank that had been used over a number of years as a marine aquarium. At that time it was thought that roofing asphalt could be used safely as a sealing material. It was heated to its melting point and poured along the inner seams of the aquarium. In this way it bridged the standard aquarium cement that oozed between the two glass sides set in the metal tank-frame and adhered to the glass on either side. Asphalt was poured along the bottom seam of the aquarium, too, where the glass sides and slate bottom meet. In this way the standard aquarium cement was completely sealed so that water could not reach it.

We had a French angelfish in this aquarium along with a four-eyed butterfly fish. After a year went by, several other fishes were added. All remained in excellent health for an additional six months. Then we began to notice that the French angel, which had grown considerably, showed faded-out areas on the black part of its body. Soon after, we discovered that the asphalt seal had separated from the seams of the tank and was no longer protecting the aquarium cement from the aquarium water. Not only was the standard aquarium cement being exposed to the water, but surfaces of the asphalt that heretofore had been intact from the water were now also exposed to it. In the years of use, the surfaces of the asphalt had gone through a leaching process and the lethal chemicals the material contains had been dispersed by constant contact with water. Now, as water seeped behind the asphalt seal, it not only came in contact with standard aquarium cement but it also bathed fresh surfaces of asphalt. It wasn't long after we discovered the large angel breathing fast that we noticed the other fishes were showing signs of distress also. Some time later all the specimens refused food. They were removed to glass jugs filled with newly collected sea water. The aquarium was broken down and new asphalt was poured along the seams after the old material had been scraped away. The French angel that we had had for the eighteen-month period was placed in a small ten-gallon tank for we felt it would offer more air surface to this big fellow than would one of the five-gallon jugs. The small tank had asphalt-sealed seams that had not been in service for any length of time. The fish died within the next few days. It was sent to a pathologist for a post-mortem examination. We received a report some time later indicating that death had been caused by exposure to toxic water. Phenol from the asphalt that had not been seasoned by long usage contaminated our aquarium water. One by one the other fishes died after they were put back into the aquarium that had only recently been renovated. This was one of the heartbreaking episodes that taught us to question the data we found on the maintenance of salt-water fishes. At that time, every booklet or article we found recommended the use of asphalt as a sealing material in one form or another.

We have worked rather closely with other aquarists and time and time again, the black or French angel has proved to be the first fish ostensibly affected when toxic conditions exist. Spots sometimes appear on these angels when neither toxicity nor parasites are the cause. Rapid respiration does not accompany them, however, and the fish behaves and eats normally. We have noted that temperature seems to be a factor here and the spots often disappear after the water has been made a few degrees warmer. Emotional upset will bring out spots occasionally. Apparently these particular spots do not indicate serious trouble, for after a while they disappear. When the spots appear and are accompanied by abnormally rapid breathing, however, the aquarist should go over his maintenance carefully to check for sources of toxicity.

Occasionally these fishes are infested with parasites. They respond very well to the copper sulfate treatment recommended in Chapter 4 in the section on disease.

A French or black angel that is in good health should be alert, its black should be smooth and glossy unless it is old enough to be losing its stripes, at which time the black fades out slightly. Its appetite should be good and its breathing comfortably slow. A recently acquired specimen should be placed in an observation tank for two weeks before release into an established aquarium.

The French and black angelfishes travel well if conditions are good. We have transferred specimens from Florida to our northern home, a distance of approximately twelve hundred miles, in our car. They were placed in aerated five-gallon glass jugs and we were careful that no extreme temperature drop occurred. This journey was made in about three days. They were in excellent condition at the end of the trip and we have never lost one in transit. They travel well by air also, when shipped properly in plastic bags, partially blown up with oxygen.

To summarize briefly on the French or black angel, we might say that these are among the most important marine tropical fishes from the aquarist's point of view. They adjust well to aquarium conditions and are peaceful if only one specimen is kept in a tank with other species. They are able to take care of themselves in the presence of aggressive fishes, they are strikingly beautiful and intelligent, and under good conditions, impressive longevity records should be possible.

Queen and Blue Angelfishes

THE blue angelfish (*Angelichthys isabelita,* Jordan and Ritter) and the queen angelfish (*Angelichthys ciliaris,* Linnaeus) differ only slightly when youngsters, the queen having perhaps a deeper shade of yellow and having a hint of an ocellus on the nape. Both of these fishes are compressed and deep. There is no problem in identifying adults as the queen has a showy ocellus on the nape which is absent on the blue angelfish. The juveniles of both species show light blue vertical stripes on dark blue or purple from the dorsal to the anal fins. The face is yellow, interrupted by a dark vertical stripe which runs from the nape, taking in the eye and passing through and below the gill plate. Both these species are found in waters off the Florida Keys and the West Indies; the blue angel is sometimes found in Bermudian waters.

Although these fishes appeal to aquarists because of their vivid blue and yellow coloring which is striking indeed, they are not nearly as satisfactory in the aquarium as the French and black angelfishes have proved to be. This is due to their belligerence, which is not only directed at one another, but at any other fish with whom they are shar-

Figure 23. QUEEN ANGELFISH (*Angelichthys ciliaris*, Linnaeus)

ing an aquarium. Even when other fishes are able to withstand their assault, no truce is made.

They adjust well to aquarium conditions and perhaps are a shade more tolerant to changing conditions than are the French and black angels. Unless the aquarist is willing to devote an aquarium exclusively to one specimen, however, of either of these fishes, he had better omit them from his collection.

Lettuce should be included in the diet unless algae have accumulated on the walls of the aquarium. They will accept raw shrimp and beef in tiny pieces and should be given regular feedings of brine shrimp. One specimen in a well-maintained aquarium will become very friendly towards its owner and makes a very fine pet.

Helen Simkatis

Figure 24. ROCK BEAUTY (*Holocanthus tricolor,* Bloch)

Rock Beauty

The rock beauty (*Holacanthus tricolor,* Bloch) is found off Bermuda, the West Indies, and sometimes the Florida Keys. It is a compressed, deep fish, resembling the angelfishes, to which it is related. Its basic color is a deep orange. The upper posterior portion of the body is black; the rest of the body is deep orange, including the long ventrals. As the fish progresses in size, the black spreads until it covers about two thirds of the body, leaving the anterior portion orange. The eyes are especially beautiful, the upper half rimmed in brilliant blue as well as the lower half. It has a small mouth that is edged in purple, giving it the appearance of wearing lipstick. A red border follows the dorsal and anal fin line and if this edging is examined closely, it will be discovered that the red is superimposed on chartreuse. Without a doubt the rock beauty is one of the most beautiful of the salt-water tropicals.

It can be well understood why the rock beauty is one of the most prized of the coral fishes indigenous to our waters. It is also one of the highest-priced fishes and to date has not been commonly owned by home aquarists. This is one of the species, however, that once established in the home aquarium will become an all-time favorite among hobbyists as it has all the attributes that make for a desirable aquarium fish. It is striking in color and design, its friendliness is almost unbelievable, it is not a bully and yet it can hold its own among specimens that tend to be. It adapts very well to almost any combination of fishes. We have never had two specimens in one aquarium but have been told that two are apt to chase one another a bit but this appears to be play rather than aggressiveness. This information comes to us from a curator of one of the large public aquariums. We have seen our own specimen chase a *Heniochus acuminatus* in what seems to be a play pattern.

The rock beauty has been treated with copper sulfate for parasites and withstood the medication without any apparent ill-effects. A white fungus was present on the edge of the anterior anal fin when we first acquired our specimen. This was treated with Lilly's tincture of Merthiolate and after several applications disappeared.

Tiny pieces of shrimp (raw and rinsed) are accepted readily. Beef, lean and in tiny pieces, serves as an alternative. Although our specimen is three inches from snout to tail, it still relishes brine shrimp. Lettuce should be supplied if algae are not established in the aquarium.

Four-Eyed Butterfly Fish

The four-eyed butterfly fish (*Chaetodon capistratus,* Linnaeus) is a compressed, deep, suborbicular fish, basically white with a faintly yellow cast, streaked with fine black broken lines that reach diagonally from the dorsal to somewhat below the lateral line where identical markings are met running up diagonally from the anal fin. A striking black band runs from the nape, encompassing the eye and passing down to the opercle. A large black ocellus appears on the sides below the posterior soft dorsal, encircled by a border of chalk white. A shadow-band occurs from the anterior spines of the dorsal to the pectoral fins and another is present from the posterior soft dorsal to a little below the ocellus. The dorsal fin, pectoral, ventral, and anal fins are shades of chrome yellow. The ventral fins are rather long, adding much interest to the fish. The mouth is small and protrudes slightly.

The fish is found in the waters off the Florida Keys, Bermuda, and the West Indies. We have collected specimens as far north as Cape Lookout, North Carolina, and it has been seen in waters off Cape Cod, but such an occurrence is quite unusual. When discovered in southern waters, it is usually accompanied by another of its kind flashing about clumps of marine plantlife or near ledges of coral beds. Its movements are erratic and on first observation, it seems to be swimming backwards, because the distinctive eyelike ocelli on the sides below the posterior dorsal are mistaken for eyes. It is a most difficult fish to catch with a hand net, for once disturbed it is very apt to veer off and disappear as competently as a flying saucer.

John Hoke

Figure 25. FOUR-EYED BUTTERFLY FISH (*Chaetodon capistratus*, Linnaeus)

The four-eyed butterfly fish is prized by aquarists because of its delicate coloring and piquant behavior. It has been kept in a closed-system aquarium for eighteen months and, like the French angelfish, there is no reason why, under ideal conditions, it can't be kept for much longer periods.

It is generally peaceful and shows only a mild aggressiveness toward its own kind. It would be a shame to keep this mannerly little fish with less gentle companions such as the blue or queen angelfishes; under such circumstances it would soon become neurotic and unhappy. Although it does well enough by itself with other tankmates, there is reason to believe that it is happier when it has a companion of its own kind. It does not adjust to aquarium conditions or fare as readily as do other coral fishes, but once established, it becomes highly satisfactory. Specimens measuring from one and a half to two inches from snout to tail are more apt to adjust to confinement than larger specimens. Growth is considerably slower than that of the angelfishes and adult size is seldom more than six inches from head to tail. In eighteen months one specimen merely doubled in size, whereas the growth of a companion French angelfish during the same period was far more dramatic.

The first food the four-eyed butterfly fish accepts is brine shrimp. Later it will take tiny pieces of raw shrimp and beef. Lettuce should be supplied if algae are not present in the aquarium. During feeding times, after it becomes accustomed to its surroundings, it will often accept a bit of food from the aquarist's fingers and hide it under a piece of coral. It will then return to join the other fishes in partaking of food for immediate consumption. Some time later, after the excitement of the feeding is over and the other fishes settle down, the butterfly will return to its hidden supply of food and quietly eat it. Sometimes it will rob a hermit crab of a morsel and occasionally it blows the tentacles of a sea anemone, daintily hunting for a tidbit that this flowerlike creature might be working toward its mouth. As the yellow-finned, black-masked bandit with exquisite movement purloins sustenance from its delicately pink, chrysanthemum-like victim, a petty theft becomes an act of grace and beauty.

We have known of a butterfly that was released into an aquarium that boasted a collection of tiny plumed tubeworms. This little fish forgot entirely that it was supposed to go through a period of adjustment, and spent the next few hours industriously dislodging the unhappy tubeworms from their calcareous casings and feasting upon them. While carrying on this orderly orgy, it reported regularly and unobtrusively with its tankmates at mealtime, and, with manners beyond reproach, accepted the tiny bits of raw shrimp its owner provided. The aquarist was at once chagrined and amused with the culprit. He glimpsed the empty tubes in the coral sadly and, oddly enough, so did the butterfly.

In its natural state, the butterfly fish is said to enter the mouths of larger fishes and remove particles of food from their teeth and clean their exteriors of parasites.

At night the butterfly dons retiring pale colors and, once settled down, it dislikes to be disturbed. It doesn't show distress when the aquarium water is chemically unbalanced as quickly as do the French angelfishes, nor does it succumb as soon. This does not indicate, however, that it is more tolerant to chemical distortion; it merely shows that the reaction comes later with the same tragic results. Despite this, however, of all the specimens treated with copper sulfate in our experiments, the four-eyed butterfly fish revealed the most discomfort when subjected to the drug. As the medication was not fatal, copper sulfate, in proportions somewhat less than those given in Chapter 4 as a standard dose, might be administered if parasites are present.

Aside from the fact that the butterfly fish is probably more timid than most reef fishes and generally more reluctant to accept aquarium conditions, it makes a fine specimen once adjusted. It is reasonably hardy, travels well by car or plane, and is extremely peaceful. Although not as spectacular as the French angelfish, it is outstandingly attractive and if its personality is quite different from other reef fishes, it has both charm and interest of its own.

Common Butterfly Fish

THE common butterfly fish (*Chaetodon ocellatus,* Bloch) is a deep, compressed fish with a dorsal fin composed of spines and rays. The dorsal, ventral, and anal fins are yellow. The body is gray on the sides,

Figure 26. COMMON BUTTERFLY FISH (*Chaetodon ocellatus,* Bloch)

blending to yellowish gray on the lower parts. The black bar, typical to butterfly fishes, originates at the anterior dorsal and runs down through the eye to the lower edge of the opercle. A black spot appears at the base of the posterior dorsal and, as though it were a drop of black ink, it runs down the body almost to the anterior anal fin. The mouth is small and protruding.

This little fish is found near coral ledges, flashing in and out of growths of marine plants. It is said to grow to eight inches in length and is found farther north than most of the coral fishes. The young have been found off the banks of North Carolina, but whether this is a common occurrence or not has not yet been established. Most specimens are collected in Florida waters.

It is hardy and some reports have described it as aggressive among its own kind. Evidence has not piled up against this little fish, however, to the extent that it should be passed by as an aquarium candidate. If the aquarist does not have an opportunity to study the specimens he intends to add to his aquarium family, it might be wise for him to settle for one specimen only.

Brine shrimp, tiny pieces of raw shrimp, and lettuce should be included in the diet.

Banded Butterfly Fish

THE banded butterfly fish (*Chaetodon striatus,* Linnaeus) is a deep, compressed, small-mouthed fish. A band originates at the nape and runs through the eye to the opercle. Vertical bands extend from the origin of the dorsal, running under the pectoral fins to abdomen and

Figure 27. BANDED BUTTERFLY FISH (*Chaetodon striatus,* Linnaeus)

from the anterior dorsal to the anal fin. Another appears faintly from the anterior of the dorsal through the peduncle.

This rather striking butterfly is found near coral ledges and sponges. It is found in the waters off Bermuda, the West Indies, and Panama. Occasionally it is discovered in waters off the Florida Keys and in isolated cases has been reported in water as far north as the Carolinas. It grows to approximately six inches from nose to tail.

This fish has proved to be a successful aquarium fish after it has become accustomed to aquarium conditions. Feeding procedure should follow that of the butterfly fishes previously mentioned. Brine shrimp is necessary, for this is the only food the fish accepts when first introduced to the aquarium.

Because the banded butterfly fish is comparatively difficult to find in Florida waters and is not nearly as common as the other butterfly fishes, it is usually quite costly.

Jewel Fish

THE marine jewel fish, sometimes called the turquoise-spotted demoiselle (*Microspathodon chrysyrus*, Cuvier and Valenciennes) is a small, deep, compressed fish. It is rather sturdily built and when less

Figure 28. MARINE JEWEL FISH
(*Microspathodon chrysyrus*, Cuvier & Valenciennes)

than three inches is black with turquoise-blue spots surrounded with lavender rings sprinkled on its sides.

It is found in waters off Bermuda and the West Indies and occasionally in southern Florida. It usually selects a hole or crevice in the coral which it guards in true demoiselle[1] fashion.

Only small specimens should be selected as these fishes are inclined to be domineering and truculent. Even when small, a specimen may prove too much for an otherwise peaceful aquarium community and

---

[1] The demoiselles are a group of little fishes that pair off in tropical waters and spend their time in a hollow, a tin can sometimes, or any type of shelter they can find. They never wander far from this home base and guard their territory against all comers with a characteristic kind of ferocity. They are so small they actually can't do much harm, but their purposeful manner belies this fact.

it is a matter of opinion whether or not the aquarist should give over a whole tank to it. Unless another aquarium is available, however, perhaps it will be wise to pass up this little star-dusted troublemaker.

Feedings of brine shrimp, raw shrimp and beef minced in tiny pieces, augmented by a substantial dry food should be included in the feeding. Lettuce should be included if algae are not present in the aquarium.

Because this fish is fairly uncommon, its usually rather high price is justified.

Sergeant Major

THE sergeant major (*Abudefduf marginatus,* Bloch) is a suborbicular, compressed fish, the back of which is yellow fading into a rather pale blue-green on the sides and blanching out to off-white on the abdomen. Six vertical bands appear on the body of the fish from the origin of the dorsal to the peduncle. The mouth is small. Adults are sometimes seen measuring approximately six inches in length.

Marine Studios, Marineland, Florida

Figure 29. SERGEANT MAJORS (*Abudefduf marginatus,* Bloch)

This little fish is a successful species and is seen in great numbers around docks and piers in Florida waters. It has been reported as far north as Rhode Island, and the author has seen specimens off Cape Lookout in North Carolina. It is common in waters off Bermuda and the West Indies.

It is one of the coral fishes that can be conditioned to low salinity and can be kept with estuary fishes if the aquarist is so inclined. It is somewhat aggressive at feeding time but is not the type of bully that will chase a tankmate down and create constant disturbance in the aquarium, as the blue angel and Beau Gregory are apt to do.

The sergeant major will eat almost anything it is offered, but should be fed as carefully as other coral fishes for good health. Such a diet includes brine shrimp, raw shrimp, raw lean beef and lettuce if algae do not appear on the walls of the aquarium. Some dry food of good quality will be eagerly accepted but, as is true of other coral fishes, this food should be regarded as a supplement rather than a staple.

Although the sergeant major can associate with estuary fishes such as the sticlebacks, puffers and killifishes, in that it can gradually adjust to brackish water, its requirements insofar as aquarium conditions are concerned are as exacting as those for other coral fishes. Many of the estuary fishes can be kept in standard aquariums but the sergeant major will not survive water that has been in contact with chemically unstable aquarium cement.

It appears on most dealers' lists and is usually quite inexpensive. Because it is hardy and reasonable in price, it is a very fine beginner's fish. By fresh-water standards it is colorful enough, but against the more vividly hued reef fishes it is somewhat inconspicuous. It holds much interest for many marine aquarists, however, because it adjusts well to aquarium conditions and can be kept with other specimens. As it never reaches more than six inches in length, it falls into the category of salt-water fishes that might well be spawned in a closed-system aquarium. Certainly its friendliness and adaptability place it among the desirables to be studied and maintained in our home aquariums.

It travels well under the conditions described in earlier chapters. It is suggested that small specimens be obtained rather than those approaching adulthood.

Although the sergeant major is one of the first little fishes the collector discovers in Florida waters, it is one of the most difficult to catch with a hand net unless a technique is developed. When in flight it swims in a zigzag course and usually escapes. It is suspicious of nets and any fast movement sends it off on some suddenly remembered mission. The tiny post-larval specimens are already equipped with a respect for danger and are as difficult to capture as their elders. This may be one reason for the success of the species.

The aquarist who is attracted to this little sparrow of the sea will be well rewarded, for it possesses all the qualities that make for a fine aquarium fish.

High Hat

THE high hat (*Pareques acuminatus*, Bloch and Schneider) has been popularly called the ribbonfish, the cluck, and the cubbyu. High hat, however, seems to be generally accepted among aquarists, and because of the eccentricity of the fish's anatomy, this is no misnomer. Its body is elongated and somewhat compressed. It has a silvery gray

Helen Simkatis

Figure 30. HIGH HAT (foreground) (*Pareques acuminatus*, Bloch and Schneider)

base with several brown to black horizontal stripes running along its body. The most predominant of these originates at the snout and runs through the eye to the apex of the caudal fin. The fish is striking because of its outlandishly high dorsal fin and long black ventrals. A soft, low dorsal appears also but is made inconspicuous by the high anterior dorsal.

The high hat is most often found in the waters off the Florida Keys, Bermuda and the West Indies, though its range is reported to be from South Carolina to Brazil. The collector usually discovers it on sandy bottoms near sponges and low-growing corals. Very small specimens are sometimes seen swimming among the long black spines of sea urchins.

This fish is usually peaceful and likes a companion of its own kind. The two will swim together and seek one another out if separated. The high hat is a bottom dweller, only coming to the surface of the water for feeding, which is a habit it acquires after it becomes adjusted to aquarium life. It finds a favorite area on the aquarium floor which it will share with one of its own kind. Although it is generally peaceful, it sometimes takes a dislike to one particular tankmate for no apparent reason. It does little more than chase this fancied adversary like a cranky old man, but the dislike is quite real and is consistently directed at the same individual.

At feeding time the high hat joins the competition for food with gusto and often explores the fingers of the aquarist for tiny bits of raw beef or raw shrimp that may be clinging to them. It nuzzles the other fishes out of the way during this operation and the aquarist becomes aware of its rough little mouth.

It would be well never to include specimens measuring less than a half-inch long with this fellow for it will probably eat them. Its tank manners on the whole are good, however, and it complements a generally peaceful aquarium community. It should not be put in the company of notorious aggressors such as the blue angel, the Beau Gregory, or the *Dascyllus,* for it would be harassed to the point of becoming neurotic and could never hold its own with such tyrants.

No longevity record has been established for this fish, although at this writing the author has one that has been doing well for eight months. The aquarium in which it is kept should always be covered (as it should be in any event) for this fish is apt to jump out of the tank if alarmed by sudden sound or movement.

It is said that specimens have been found measuring a foot in length. The rate of growth apparently is slow, however, and it would take a long time for a specimen of from one to two inches in length to outgrow an aquarium of a thirty-five-gallon capacity.

The diet of the high hat includes small pieces of raw shrimp and lean beef. It will accept chopped and cleaned earthworms and occasionally likes dry food. Although it eats brine shrimp as do most of the coral fishes, it must have more substantial fare such as that which we have mentioned above.

The high hat will not tolerate chemically distorted water and requires the exacting conditions in the aquarium demanded by all the salt-water tropicals. It has survived the copper sulfate treatment, however, without any visible signs of discomfort. It travels well by automobile and plane if prepared for shipment in the manner previously prescribed for coral fishes in earlier chapters. Under no condition should this fish be crowded as it is highly sensitive to water low in oxygen content.

Although the high hat has been described in other books as shy and delicate, we have found it to be quite at home in the aquarium and hardy if conditions are good. Because of its ridiculously high dorsal and long black ventral fins, it is attractive and has much in its favor to make it desirable.

Cardinal Fish

The cardinal fish (*Apogon sellicauda,* Evermann and Marsh) is a small, compressed, somewhat elongated fish with rather a large mouth and eyes. As is true in the cases of many of the coral fishes, there are several kinds of cardinal fishes but the *Apogon sellicauda* is the variety that appears most commonly on dealers' lists and the one most often collected by aquarists who catch their own specimens. As its popular name suggests, it is scarlet, with a black spot on the opercle which continues forward across the eye, bordered narrowly with neon blue-green. There are two dorsal fins, the anterior being spinous and the

Marine Studios, Marineland, Florida

Figure 31. CARDINAL FISH (*Apogon sellicauda*. Evermann and Marsh)

posterior soft. A black spot appears below the rear portion of the soft dorsal and another smudgelike saddle is present on the caudal peduncle.

It is found in waters off Bermuda, the West Indies and the Florida Keys. The large eyes suggest that this fish might be a nocturnal feeder but it shows up at mealtimes during the day with its tank-mates in the aquarium.

Collectors discover the cardinal on sandy bottoms near low coral beds and sponges. Very small specimens are sometimes found swimming among the long black spines of sea urchins.

It adjusts to aquarium life rather quickly and will accept small pieces of raw shrimp, beef, and cut and cleaned earthworms. It likes brine shrimp and occasionally will take dry food.

The cardinal is a peaceful little fish and should not be introduced into an aquarium that includes blue angels, Beau Gregories and other such aggressors.

It is thought that aquarium fare may exclude a food important to it which is available to it only in its natural habitat. After a few months in the aquarium, the cardinal seems to backslide and finally it dies quietly, without any particular sign of distress. For this reason alone the aquarist might well pass up this beautiful little red fish until further data is established as to its dietary needs.

Royal Gramma

The royal gramma is listed as *Gramma loreto* (Poey) in the *Check List of the Fishes of North and Middle America* by Jordan, Evermann and Clark and is given in the *Field Book of Shore Fishes of Bermuda* by

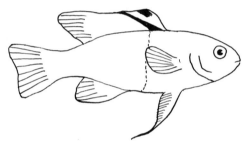

Figure 32. ROYAL GRAMMA (*Gramma hemichrysos,* Mowbray)

Beebe and Tee-Van as *Gramma Hemichrysos* (Mowbray). Beebe and Tee-Van state that this species can be easily confused with the young Spanish hogfish (*Bodianus rufus*) which it resembles very closely.

It has been popularly called the blue and gold fairy basslet but now the popular name generally accepted is the royal gramma. It is a small, somewhat compressed, elongated fish, strikingly marked. The anterior is a bright vermilion to purple and the posterior part of the body shows bright yellow to orange.

There isn't very much information available on this little flame-like fish, probably because it is usually listed at high prices and few hobbyists have owned it. Neither is it a fish for the amateur collector for it is reportedly found only in deep water off the outer reefs of the West Indies and the Florida Keys.

A difference of opinion exists as to its hardiness, some reports indicating that it is extremely delicate and others suggesting it thrives in captivity. We mention it here merely to point out to the aquarist who aspires to own it that such a venture is of the pioneer variety and that its high cost makes it rather a bad risk.

We have seen it in the company of other fishes and it appears to be peaceful in disposition. Its breath-taking beauty is enough to make any salt-water aquarist forget its high cost, and its gentle tank manners tilt the scales in its favor.

For the aquarist who cannot resist this beauty, we suggest that small pieces of raw shrimp and beef should make up the important portion of the royal gramma's diet; it is reported to relish a baby guppy occasionally. Lettuce should be offered if algae are not present on the walls of the aquarium.

Neon Goby

The neon goby (*Elacatinus oceanops,* Jordan) is an elongated fish with a neon-blue stripe running from the snout to tail, on a black to gray base.

It is found in waters off the Florida Keys and the West Indies. The adults are said to be up to three and a half inches from snout to tail.

It adjusts to aquarium life very well but should be bought or collected in pairs. A compatible couple can be selected by a brief study. These two little fishes are inseparable and can be seen in their natural habitat or in an aquarium moving in and out of holes in the coral, a kind of game of hide-and-seek that goes on constantly. They tame very soon after capture and the aquarist who offers tiny pieces of food from his fingers will be surprised to feel these featherlike little creatures exploring his hand with their inimitable gliding movements.

They have a specialized set of ventral fins which enable them to move over vertical surfaces with little difficulty. Often they ride tankmates, apparently seeking external parasites. If none are present they move off with a somewhat disappointed air. When their tankmates invite this sort of thing constantly, the aquarist should begin

Helen Simkatis

Figure 33. NEON GOBY (*Elacatinus oceanops,* Jordan)

This little fish can be seen resting on a piece of coral rock. A dwarf sea horse (*Hippocampus zosterae,* Jordan and Gilbert), anchored to a gorgonian skeleton, seems to be interested in his tankmate.

to suspect that some sort of parasite has infested his specimens. The gobies will not remain long on a fish that is clean.

The neon goby has proved to be one of the most successful salt-water aquarium fishes. Although they are naturally hardy, good conditions must prevail, for they are subject to parasites and sensitive to chemically unbalanced salt water, as are any of the other marine tropicals. When conditions are right, these little fishes compete with their tankmates for food by coming to the surface of the water at feeding time. They are so small that unless care is taken that they get their share, they are left out. A successful feeding routine seems to be to allow the most aggressive fishes to eat their fill and then see that the shy specimens are satisfied. The gobies like tiny pieces of raw shrimp and beef and eagerly feed on brine shrimp when it is present. If algae are not present on the walls of the aquarium, minute bits of lettuce should be offered.

Neon gobies that are healthy and contented are active and make very fine exhibits. When they keep out of sight, they are either unhappy because of a tank bully or they are not up to par physically.

Only one compatible pair should be introduced into an aquarium as an outsider is often persecuted by a mated pair and two pairs are apt to quarrel over territorial rights.

There have been many reports of these little fishes spawning in closed-system aquariums. The fry have usually died off as a result of a nutritional deficiency. If the aquarist is lucky enough to have such an event take place in his tank, he might remove the breeding pair to an aquarium by themselves, one that has a good growth of algae on its walls. When ready to spawn, these little fishes prepare a spot under a piece of coral or some other secluded place by cleaning sand and debris away. The eggs are layed and fertilized after the courtship. In an aquarium where algae are present, microscopic animal life accompanies them. These tiny little creatures could well serve as food for the fry until they are able to take brine shrimp. Freshly hatched brine shrimp should be offered several times a day in any event, so that it will be present when the fry are able to take it. If the babies seem to be dying off alarmingly fast, it might be a good idea to destroy some of them in order that the existing microscopic food will be plentiful enough to nourish a few rather than be stretched inadequately among a great many. In this way some of the youngsters may be saved.

From every point of view the neon goby is satisfactory for the home aquarium. It is colorful and has a great deal of personality. It should not be included in an aquarium where truculent species such as the blue angel, the Beau Gregory, or *Dascyllus trimaculatus* are present, nor should it be kept with specimens measuring over three and a half inches from head to tail.

Queen Triggerfish

The queen triggerfish (*Balistes vetula,* Linnaeus) is a compressed fish with leatherlike skin. Scales are evident, however, upon close examination. The dorsal fin is divided, the first portion composed of three spines. The anterior spine is the highest and heaviest of these.

The posterior dorsal is soft and gracefully trailing. The caudal fin is exaggerated and concave; the tips are somewhat streamer-like. Two broad curving bands of blue cross the cheeks of this fish with several narrower bands above them. There are painted eyelash markings around the rather large blue eyes. The basic color of the fish is a varying rich yellowish brown.

This fish is usually found in waters off Bermuda, the West Indies and the Florida Keys; it has been reported as far north as Massachusetts. It grows to about fifteen inches in length.

The queen triggerfish is one of the most striking specimens displayed at Marineland, the oceanarium in Florida, and the aquarist who is attracted by its bizarre shape and brilliant markings might very well seek it out on his dealer's list. For some reason, small specimens are not seen even in public aquariums and this may account for the fact that little is known as to how it adjusts to aquarium conditions.

If the aquarist finds a specimen of this showy fish that he can accommodate, he might very well acquire it, for the small mouth would indicate that it will accept small pieces of raw shrimp and beef and not be a threat to other fishes. Such a venture will be of a pioneering nature, however, for no written account of its being kept in a home

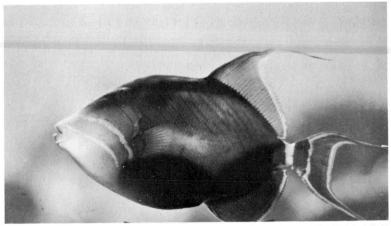

Marine Studios, Marineland, Florida

Figure 34. QUEEN TRIGGERFISH (*Balistes vetula,* Linnaeus)

aquarium has been unearthed by this writer. In all such experiments, it is desirable to include lettuce in the diet if algae are not present, as vegetation is an important food to most of the salt water tropicals. It is also wise to watch a fish for tank manners on which little data is available. Although the queen triggerfish may be a perfect lady in company, the sharp teeth that protrude slightly beyond the fish's small mouth could be a vicious weapon.

Filefishes

The common filefish (*Stephanolepis hispidus,* Linnaeus) is a small, leathery fish with a high dorsal spine just behind the nape. The body is often a mottled green but the fish is subject to frequent color change, from varying shades of green to gray. The very young specimens are sometimes a bright green. The mouth is small and the teeth minute and sharp.

There are several types of filefishes occurring all along the Atlantic coast. Sometimes the young are found in the grassy bottoms of

Marine Studios, Marineland, Florida

Figure 35. SCRAWLED FILEFISH (*Alutera scripta,* Osbeck)

estuaries. They all have the single-spined dorsal in common and the grotesque line from snout to pelvic spine, varying in shape from concave to convex and in some species, such as the *Stephanolepis hispidus,* being almost straight.

These are hardy little fishes and do very well in the aquarium. Specimens measuring less than an inch from snout to tail, however, are said to damage the eyes of larger fishes by picking at them. The larger specimens measuring over three inches from snout to tail are rather hard on hermit crabs. Probably a hermit crab that takes a shell somewhat smaller than a table-tennis ball can hold his own with these fellows, but smaller hermits usually are not able to withstand the attack.

The filefishes are voracious eaters and will accept raw beef, raw shrimp, and brine shrimp. The aquarist who fancies a collection of tube worms or barnacles in his tank will find these prizes ravished shortly after he introduces the bright green little filefish he caught on his collecting trip.

Filefishes are very easily captured by either dredging a grassy bottom with a seine or scooping up clumps of sargassum weed in a net while drifting along in a boat. These will usually be tiny specimens. The larger specimens are often picked up by fishermen working with large seines or shrimp nets, who are, as a rule, quite ready to turn them over to an aquarist who happens to be on the scene.

For the aquarist who does not wish to go in for the more delicate coral fishes, the filefishes make interesting aquarium pets that demand little more than a good diet and a clean aquarium.

Cowfish

The cowfish (*Acanthostracion quadricornis,* Linnaeus) is encased in bony armor. The ventral ridge diminishes to a terminal spine and a hornlike spine appears over each rather large eye, giving this little fish a somewhat bovine head structure. The caudal, dorsal, pectoral and anal fins protrude through perforations in the bony covering of the body, and it is only through the movement of these that propulsion is possible, the encased body of the fish being rigid.

The coloring varies but usually broken blue horizontal stripes are

Figure 36. COWFISH (*Acanthostracion quadricornis,* Linnaeus)

interspersed with yellow of a similar irregular pattern. Brown blotches are superimposed over these. When sun or artificial light hit the blue, it becomes vivid and the general appearance of the fish is quite striking. The mouth protrudes slightly and is small.

These little fishes are found from the Carolinas to Brazil and occasionally are reported as far north as Massachusetts. They occur on grassy flats and are collected by seining or dredging. Large specimens often surprise collectors as they spin by them across sandy flats at a speed that is so unexpected from them that they are often mistaken for another kind of fish.

They adjust rather well to aquarium conditions if they are acquired while still measuring less than two inches from head to tail. Their movements are slow and their temperament quiet. They should be kept with tankmates of their own kind or in generally peaceful aquarium communities. A blue angel would make life rather difficult for one of these gentle fishes.

They reach a length of something over nine inches when adult.

Specimens measuring approximately four inches are often available to aquarists but, of course, should not be accepted, as specimens this large seldom adjust to aquarium conditions.

Brine shrimp, tiny pieces of raw shrimp and beef will be accepted by these little fellows and lettuce should be supplied if algae are not present in the aquarium.

Although the coloring of these odd little creatures of the sea is very interesting, it is their unusual structure that accounts for the popularity they enjoy among aquarists.

Blue Tang

The blue tang (*Acanthurus caeruleus,* Bloch and Schneider) is a compressed, somewhat deep fish. The dorsal fin originates just behind the

Marine Studios, Marineland, Florida

Figure 37. TANGS (*Acanthurus caeruleus,* Bloch and Schneider)

nape and follows the round shape of the body as does the anal fin. The mouth is small and slightly protruding. On either side of the body near the peduncle is a strong, sharp-edged and pointed spine that can be erected when the fish is in danger and used as a slashing weapon. The species is blue as both its scientific and vernacular names suggest but the fish is subject to considerable color change and fade-out.

The tang is found in waters off Bermuda, Florida, the West Indies and Brazil. It is one of a successful family and is fairly common. The adults measure somewhat over a foot in length.

The possibility of the tang using the sharp, razorlike weapon with which it is equipped on its tankmates when in fear or anger has frightened most aquarists away even though the fish is strikingly beautiful.

Reports on its adjustment to aquarium conditions have been few and those have been discouraging. There is no reason why this fish could not be kept in an aquarium by itself, however, and its attractiveness would warrant such an experiment. Raw beef and shrimp in tiny pieces should be offered along with a supplement of lettuce should algae not be present in the aquarium.

Bluehead

The bluehead (*Thalassoma bifasciatus,* Bloch) is an elongated, spindle-shaped, small-mouthed fish. It is one of the many beautiful wrasses[1] that are common in warm seas. The tail is rounded in small specimens and deeply concave in adults, the males having rather exaggerated tips. Coloration varies among individuals but the adult male has a blue head followed by two vertical black bands divided by blue. The posterior portion of the body is a blue green. The females are only different from the young specimens in size and do not have the distinctive vertical bands. The base color is a vivid yellow or lime. A narrow brown stripe originates at the snout and passes through the eye to the pectoral fin. It continues again in a wide lateral band behind the base of the pectoral fin and may or may not be broken. A

---

[1] The wrasses are a group of fishes that are generally found in tropical waters. They are oblong or elongate and are equipped with strong, caninelike jaw teeth and powerful pharyngeal teeth with which they crush mollusks. Some break off chunks of coral and eat the crustacea and polyps imbedded in it. They are usually brightly colored.

stripe appears on the anterior dorsal and the edges of the caudal fin are bordered in black. These fishes can change color rapidly. The adults are seldom seen longer than six inches from snout to tail. The occur in waters off the West Indies, the Florida Keys and Bermuda. They are found swimming about coral reefs in search of small animal life on which they feed.

The young form a bubble around them when they sleep which serves as a protection from intruders. If the bubble is broken, they can move off to quieter quarters. The adults sleep on their sides, half buried in the sandy bottom, and will take over a whelk shell in an aquarium if one is supplied.

The Smithsonian Institution

Figure 38. BLUEHEAD (*Thalassoma bifasciatus*, Bloch)

The unusual color patterns of these fishes make them especially attractive to aquarists. Actually, they do not adjust well to aquarium conditions. They swim back and forth in the aquarium in a restless manner which is disturbing to other better adjusted tankmates.

If the aquarist chooses to overlook this mannerism, and acquires one of these colorful fishes, he should supply adult brine shrimp, small pieces of lean beef, and lettuce should be offered if algae are not present. In the writer's opinion, however, fishes that are not contented in an aquarium are best omitted.

Spiny Boxfish

The spiny boxfish (*Chilomycterus schoepfii*, Walbaum) is a sturdy fish in structure, and the body is covered with broad-based rigid spines. It has dark linear markings somewhat undulating on a yellowish-green background which varies in shade. An ocellated spot appears below the dorsal which is soft and placed on the anterior portion of the body.

Figure 39. SPINY BOXFISH (*Chilomycterus schoepfii,* Walbaum)

Ocellated spots appear just behind the pectoral fins. Ventral fins are lacking. The fish is especially attractive to aquarists because of its widely spaced, conspicuously blue eyes.

These fishes, like the puffers and porcupine fishes, to which they are related, are capable of blowing up when alarmed or handled. The spiny boxfish is not as subject to this reflex as the puffers and porcupine fishes are apt to be. When handled, however, it makes a rasping, croak-like sound.

This fish is found in southern waters along the Atlantic coast. We have seen adults in waters off Virginia and they have been occasionally reported as far north as Cape Cod.

Specimens of this species have been caught infested with *Oödinium,* the parasitic dinoflagellate, and the aquarist should be especially careful to isolate a recently acquired specimen of this attractive fish for at least three weeks before introducing it into a healthy aquarium. (See Chapter 4 on disease for recommended treatment.)

The spiny boxfish is an amiable, peaceful fellow and becomes quite tame. Aquarists become very fond of individual specimens, and such pets are usually hand-fed and named. This fish will not usually become aggressive but should not be included with specimens considerably smaller than it. On the other hand, it should not be expected to compete with such notorious aggressors as the blue angel and the Beau Gregory.

In its natural state, it hunts for tube worms and tiny shrimp, its strong, sharp teeth quite able to crush calcareous formations. In the aquarium, the usual fare of tiny pieces of beef, raw shrimp, and brine shrimp is accepted. The aquarists who live near the sea might supplement this diet by occasionally collecting a supply of the tiny shrimp that are found in seaweed.

This interesting little fish is an appropriate member for an aquarium community that is made up of peaceful specimens comparable to it in size. It should never be placed in a tank that is heavily populated for, due to some metabolic peculiarity, it is said to give off more waste materials than other fishes.

Sargassum Fish

The sargassum fish (*Histrio histrio*) is probably one of the most interesting examples of mimicry in nature, a subject that fascinates most people. It appears to be an animated bit of the sargassum weed in which it lives and through this permanent disguise it has lived well and has become a most successful species. Clumps of sargassum weed break away from the vast masses that float in the famous Sargasso Sea, and are carried by the currents toward the southeastern shores of our country, bringing with them a host of tiny creatures. The clumps of weed sometimes are washed into shore with the tide only to be swept seaward again when the waves recede. A piece that we may pick up today along the water's edge may be well out to sea sometime tomorrow, taking its many small passengers with it.

Among the creatures found aboard this unusual vessel is one that

Figure 40. SARGASSUM FISH (*Histrio histrio*)

resembles the weed itself so much that unless we catch a clump in a net and place it in a pail of water, rinsing and discarding each washed-out piece of weed as we go, we would never find it. Even in an aquarium a single sargassum fish often resembles a scrap of sea-weed that is there by mistake.

Examining the sargassum fish closely, we discover it is an animated caricature of a fish. The nape is a base for two weedlike appendages, the first one being the shorter. The dorsal is present but seems like a bit of weed growing from the back of the fish. The pectoral, ventral, anal and caudal fins are present but modified to blend in with the general make-up of the fish.

Its markings and coloring match the sargassum weed so perfectly, that even the little air sacs that keep the weed afloat seem to be present. The camouflage is not used as a defense but as a disguise for catching unsuspecting prey, and seldom does a small fish or shrimp escape when once stalked by this harmless-appearing predator.

The sargassum fish is found in the southern waters of the Atlantic, sometimes venturing as far north as Cape Hatteras on its constantly moving ferry.

The aquarist who likes the unusual might well set up an aquarium for this grotesque fellow who cannot be kept with other fishes because of its voracious appetite. We have caught several on occasion to arrive home with only one suffernig from a very bad case of indigestion. The sargassum fish plays no favorites—another fish, sibling or not, is just something to eat.

It demands the same requirements as other marine tropicals and has been kept in aquariums for substantial lengths of time. A very fine article appears in *The Aquarium,* December, 1955, by Dr. Myron Gordon entitled "Histrio—The Fish on the Sargasso Sea Merry-Go-Round." In this a spawning is described in detail. Apparently none of the young survived.

It is doubtful whether the sargassum fish would accept other than live food, a point that might discourage many aquarists.

Dwarf Sea Horse

The dwarf sea horse (*Hippocampus zosterae,* Jordan and Gilbert) is the smallest sea horse and the most successful of the sea horses in the home aquarium. It does not reach over two inches in length and is found in the Gulf of Mexico and on the flats off the Florida Keys.

Of all the marine fishes, perhaps the sea horse has received the most attention. Articles, books, and moving pictures have revealed much of their mysterious little lives to us. Despite the literature available on them, we still have people ask us confidentially: "Is there really such a fish?" Without a doubt, there is something in the design of the sea horse that is reminiscent of the creatures that have evolved from man's imagination, such as the centaurs, fauns and dragons. The head is quite like that of a horse and the arching neck furthers the resemblance. From there on, however, the sea horse is on its own. The body is covered with a bony material which is lined off to resemble plate armor. The dorsal appears just above where the body and tail meet. The tail is as long as the head and body combined, and tapers to a point. It is prehensile and used for anchoring to grasses or whatever else is available. The eyes move independently of each other. The *Hippo-*

campus zosterae is usually a light warm brown, but the color varies, sometimes fading to an off-white.

The breeding habits of the sea horse are a feature that surprises and amuses its admirers and the very most is made of it by the writers for Sunday supplements and popular magazines. The female, during the nuptual embrace, inserts her ovipositor into the brood pouch of the male and deposits her eggs there. When the incubation period is completed, the male goes through a series of spastic movements, after which the young horses are spewed out of the pouch opening.

We have watched this occur in our sea horse tank when several other specimens were present. None of the adults made an attempt to harm the babies who sank to the bottom of the aquarium. Within

Helen Simkatis

Figure 41. DWARF SEA HORSE (*Hippocampus zosterae,* Jordan and Gilbert)

a few minutes some were swimming about and others had found anchorage on their father's head and various other parts of his body. This tank had algae growing on the walls among which certain kinds of microscopic animals are usually present. We were afraid, however, that the supply would not feed all the active fry which were, we thought, too small to take freshly hatched brine shrimp. We removed all but ten of the youngsters and it was shortly after this that we learned that they were able to take newly hatched brine shrimp. Of the ten babies, we raised six. They all live quite happily with the three original adults in a ten-gallon Plexiglas tank.

The aquarium should contain a small lump of coral and the skeleton of a gorgonian sea whip should be included for anchorage. Brine shrimp is the staple of these little creatures and it should be supplied once a day at least. They eat frequently and as this seems to be the only food they will accept, it should be plentiful.

The dwarf sea horse is the most successful type of this fascinating fish in the home aquarium. It settles down to aquarium life very well and does not seem to yearn for its natural habitat. Other varieties of the sea horse do not adjust and curators of public aquariums seem to account for the fact as being a "humoral," or psychological, factor.

The sea horse moves slowly and seems to require tranquillity. To include with it even a pipefish—its near-relative—is a mistake.

Northern and Bermuda Sea Horses

The northern sea horse (*Hippocampus hudsonius,* De Kay) and the Bermuda sea horse (*Hippocampus punctulatus,* Guichenot) are available to aquarists quite frequently. The northern variety is found from South Carolina to Cape Cod in the coastal waters on grassy bottoms during the summer months. In the winter it disappears and its whereabouts during that period is unknown. It attains from five to seven inches in length when adult. The Bermuda sea horse is found from North Carolina to Tortuga on weed-covered bottoms of coastal waters. It attains about five inches when adult, although occasionally it is found seven inches from snout to tail.

The bony plates of the Bermuda sea horse are smaller than those of

Marine Studios, Marineland, Florida

Figure 42. BERMUDA SEA HORSE (*Hippocampus punctulatus*, Guichenot)—father and progeny.

the northern type and the dorsal is smaller. The snout is not as blunt nor as thick but both varieties are attractive and their aquarium manners similar.

The breeding habits resemble those of the dwarf sea horse but the young are said not to be able to take freshly hatched brine shrimp. A fusion of algae-green water should be introduced into the aquarium if birth of young occurs. There has been no account of a breeding that actually took place in the aquarium, although males already bearing young have released them after capture.

Neither fish usully accepts food unless it is alive. Brine shrimp, baby guppies and baby mollies are accepted. Both varieties fail to settle down to aquarium life as well as the dwarf sea horse does. They require a tank to themselves as the presence of other kinds of fishes seems to upset them.

A piece of coral should be present in their aquarium, which should be gently aerated. They should be supplied a gorgonian skeleton for anchoring purposes. Feedings must be scheduled regularly as they have vigorous appetites when first captured. As long as they take interest in food the aquarist does not have to worry about them. They have been kept from six months to a year in aquariums but as time goes on, they seem to lose interest in food and in life as a whole. Complete apathy finally sets in and they eventually die quietly. Their failure as aquarium specimens seems to be purely psychological.

Grunts

The grunts of the family Haemulidae are mentioned here merely to explain why, although they are small, colorful, and available, they should not be included in the home aquarium.

These little fishes frequent the southern littoral waters in large schools, swimming about docks and piers. Further out, they haunt the coral beds and sponges, always in motion, and always traveling from one place to another. Skin divers meet them while swimming along the sandy bottom of the ocean floor and are amused by their curiosity. The very nature of these little wanderers, however, prevents them from ever adjusting to aquarium life even when the conditions are ideal. In

Marine Studios, Marineland, Florida

Figure 43. BLUE-STRIPED GRUNT (*Haemulon sciurus,* Shaw)

captivity, they pace back and forth in the aquarium and, although they accept food, it never seems to give them the nourishment they require. Usually they prosper for a while and then sink into a decline from which they never recover.

The novice collector will be attracted by the striking design of the blue-striped grunt. Swim with these little fishes and enjoy their company in their natural habitat but leave them there, for it is only in the southern seas that they retain their beauty and vitality.

Recommended Reading

Charles M. Breder, Jr., *Field Book of Marine Fishes of the Atlantic Coast,* Putnam, 1948.

William Beebe and John Tee-Van, *Field Book of the Shore Fishes of Bermuda,* Putnam, 1933.

Walter H. Chute, *Guide to the John G. Shedd Aquarium,* 1953.

David Star Jordan, Barton Warren Evermann and Howard Walton Clark, *Check List of the Fishes and Fishlike Vertebrates of North and Middle America North of the Northern Boundary of Venezuela and Colombia,* U. S. Government Printing Office, 1955.

CHAPTER 8

The Exotics[1]

Clownfish

The clownfish (*Amphiprion percula,* Lacépède), sometimes referred to as the anemone fish, has probably attracted more aquarists to the salt-water hobby than any other marine tropical species. It has so much in its favor by way of interest, color, personality, and adaptability as an aquarium fish, a hobbyist could well afford to confine his attention to this beautiful little fish alone.

The spindle-shaped body is basically a brilliant orange with broad chalk-white vertical bands, accented by narrow velvet black borders. The first band originates at the nape, the second takes in the center of the dorsal and girdles the body, the band taking on points, the apexes of which are hidden under the pectoral fins. The third band crosses the caudal peduncle. The fins are rounded and often edged in black, although some individuals do not show black on the dorsal or ventral fins.

Writers have occasionally voiced objection to the vernacular designation of clownfish for this species, but as the color pattern of no other fish follows that of the traditional costume of clowns so closely, we feel that the name is appropriate.

These little fishes are found in the coral reefs of Ceylon and throughout the Indo-Pacific. They are symbiotic with the anemones of the

---

[1] We have referred to this group of fishes as the *exotics,* as they are not indigenous to waters off the United States.

Helen Simkatis

Figure 44. CLOWNFISH (*Amphiprion percula*)

genera Stoichatis and Discosoma, either of which may have a diameter from sixteen to twenty-four inches. These anemones have cells in their many tentacles which are capable of stinging a small fish to death. The clownfish, however, swims in and out of these graceful tentacles with impunity and from time to time drops tidbits to its symbiont as though rewarding it for its consideration. A pair will nest within arm's length of an anemone and under this protection rear a family. Both parents care for the eggs. The female is usually considerably larger than her mate. The young are gray the first two weeks of their lives and then assume the coloration of their parents.

The clownfishes are among the most dramatic of the marine fishes, not only for their brilliant coloring and interesting design but also for their winsome personality. They delight their owners as they wave their rounded pectoral fins and rock back and forth in a manner characteristic of them alone. They tame easily and eagerly accept food from the fingers. They are completely successful aquarium fishes which, of course, adds to their popularity among hobbyists. A mated pair of clowns lived in a closed-system aquarium in this country for seven years, a truly remarkable record for either fresh- or salt-water fishes. This pair spawned many times but none of the young were saved. Later, another aquarist succeeded in raising nine youngsters. In three months, however, all had died except one. Diet is probably one of the important factors in raising salt-water fry. When the young are able to take brine shrimp, the feedings should be frequent. A very suitable food for newly hatched babies is a tiny creature always prevalent in the algae that grow on the coral and walls of the aquarium. A tank that contains water that is slightly green from suspended algae would be particularly desirable for a breeding pair of clowns. Next best would be to add water to the aquarium from an aerated glass jug that has been standing in sunlight for some time.

Clownfishes are shipped into the United States regularly and arrive in excellent condition. When in good health, their respiration is slow and their fins are spread out. An indication that conditions in an aquarium are good is expressed by their response to a motion of a hand and by their general alertness. They must be kept in water that is chemically balanced but on a whole they are hardy little fishes. They have survived the copper sulfate treatment when attacked by *Oödinium,* and other external parasites.

They accept small pieces of lean beef and raw shrimp and relish brine shrimp. Lettuce should be offered daily if algae are absent in the aquarium. Dry food of a good quality may be offered occasionally.

After a pair has become established in an aquarium, additional specimens of the same species should not be introduced. Although they are never aggressive to other species of fishes, an established pair will make others of their own kind feel unwanted in a surprisingly vigorous manner. They usually take over a station in the aquarium and swim in a limited area in a rocking motion which is accelerated when they are alarmed and just before retiring time at dusk. A favorite place in the aquarium is near a piece of coral that is formed so that it offers hiding places. Dead rock coral perforated in several places is ideal.

The adults are approximately three and a half inches in length from snout to tail and they do not lose their beautiful coloring as they grow older. The rate of growth is rather slow. If small specimens are selected, the aquarist can be reasonably sure that they are not advanced in age.

It is not necessary to obtain an anemone (of the genera Stoichatis or Discosoma) to keep these little fishes happy, although such an introduction would make for an interesting aquarium. If either of these species of anemones were acquired, no other species of fishes could be included in the tank with the exception of the *Dascyllus trimaculatus* or *Dascyllus Aruanus.* Other species are not tolerated by these anemones. Such an aquarium would have to be of a seventy- or eighty-gallon capacity, as these anemones have a diameter of from sixteen to twenty-four inches, as mentioned previously.

The remarkable longevity records that have been achieved by aquarists with *Amphiprion percula* were made without anemones present. The beautiful anemone found in Florida waters, *Condylactus passiflora,* does not attract these little fishes, we have heard, although we have never attempted the experiment ourselves.

Amphiprion percula, without a doubt, has received more attention from aquarists than any other species of the marine tropicals. It has everything in its favor to hold the interest of the hobbyist and, as the popularity of the marine tropicals grows, we are sure that we will hear that some skillful aquarist has raised a family of these lovely little creatures.

Amphiprion Bicinctus (Ruppell)

The *Amphiprion bicinctus* is popularly called a clownfish, probably because it belongs to the family Amphiprionidae and somewhat resembles *Amphiprion percula.* Perhaps as this species becomes better known among aquarists, it will gain a popular name based on its own personality rather than on that of its relative.

This fish is basically a brown which fades to pink and finally to yellow on the undersides. Three blue-white vertical bands are present on the body, the first originating in front of the dorsal and running to the opercle; the second begins at the posterior dorsal and extends to the anterior anal, the third saddles the caudal peduncle. The fins are yellowish and darken with age. There are considerable variations in color among individuals but in any phase the fish is strikingly beautiful. It attains six inches in length when adult, and is found throughout the coastal waters of the tropical Indo-Pacific.

The *Amphiprion bicinctus* adapts very well to aquarium conditions and although it is not as well known as the *percula,* reports would lead us to believe that it will in time become as popular among aquarists. Its needs and requirements are similar to those of the *percula.*

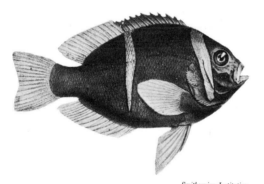

Smithsonian Institution

Figure 45. *AMPHIPRION BICINCTUS* (Ruppell)

Dascyllus Trimaculatus (Ruppell)

The *Dascyllus trimaculatus* is a sturdy, compressed, somewhat orbicular, small-mouthed fish. Species measuring from one half to two and a half inches from snout to tail are black with a white spot on either side of the body, just below the eighth or ninth dorsal spine. Another white spot appears on the nape. The spots on the sides remain when the fish becomes adult (three and a half inches), but the spot on the nape gradually disappears and the black fades to brown. Only the ventral fins, which are rather long, remain black.

Helen Simkatis

Figure 46. *DASCYLLUS TRIMACULATUS*

Because of the conspicuous white spots on the basic black of the young specimens, there has been a feeble tendency among aquarists and dealers to call this fish the *domino*. It is more often referred to, however, as the three-spotted *Dascyllus;* the complete scientific name is also quite frequently used.

This fish is found in coastal waters throughout the tropical Indo-

Pacific. It is said to be symbiotic with the anemone *Actinia equina*, as is the clownfish (*Amphiprion percula*).

The *Dascyllus trimaculatus* is probably one of the hardiest of the marine tropicals and adjusts very well to aquarium conditions. It is infamously aggressive, however, and should not be kept with specimens that cannot compete with it, such as the high hat, the neon goby and others. It will bully any fish that retreats under its attack.

This fish has been kept for a year in artificial salt water (Neptune Salts) and for several years in natural sea water. Under good conditions it seems to thrive in the aquarium. A specimen measuring slightly under an inch from head to tail grew to two and a half inches in eleven months.

Although exceptionally hardy, the *Dascyllus trimaculatus* will not tolerate chemically unbalanced water. It has, however, withstood the copper sulfate treatment. We have two specimens which were infested with *Oödinium,* the parasitic dinoflagellate. They responded to the copper sulfate treatment very well and were rid of the parasite in twelve hours. At this writing, two years later, these fishes are in top condition.

The *Dascyllus trimaculatus* have spawned in a closed-system aquarium and the method of egg-laying resembles that of the fresh-water ciclids. A spot is chosen and cleaned, and the eggs are cared for by both parents who fan them with their pectoral fins constantly. Although the eggs hatched successfully, the young died apparently from a nutritional deficiency.

As the *Dascyllus trimaculatus* takes over a section of the aquarium and is very possessive of a piece of coral or a shell, one or the other should be present in the aquarium. Although it guards its home base carefully, it has no qualms about invading territories claimed by other specimens. When excited, this little fish makes a sharp chirping sound that is quite audible outside the tank. It pales out on occasion when emotionally aroused and dark blue areas appear on the dorsal and caudal fins.

Brine shrimp and tiny pieces of raw shrimp and lean beef should be offered, supplemented by small pieces of lettuce if algae are not present in the aquarium. It is a hearty eater and apt to intimidate its tankmates during feeding time. We usually allow our specimens to take as much food as they want and after we are sure they are completely satisfied, we feed their tankmates.

If its tankmates are selected carefully, the *Dascyllus trimaculatus* can be kept with other fishes. Usually larger specimens than it should be chosen, with the exception of the clownfishes. For some reason the clowns are seldom attacked by this miscreant. Because it is both interesting and attractive, it is quite worthy of being set up in an aquarium with only another of its kind present. Its hardiness, adaptability to aquarium conditions and attractiveness make it an important salt-water aquarium fish.

Dascyllus Aruanus (Linnaeus)

The *Dascyllus aruanus* is a compressed, suborbicular fish with three wide vertical black bands on the body, which is basically a pearly

Figure 47. *DASCYLLUS ARUANUS*

white. The first band originates at the nape, encompassing the eye and including the lips, leaving a white patch just above the snout. The second runs from the anterior dorsal to the ventral fins, and the third from the posterior dorsal to the anal. The ventral fins are rather long and as black as the bands on the body. The dorsal and pectoral fins are black. The general shape and markings of this fish are especially attractive, suggestive of what an artist's idea of a little fish for a child's storybook might be.

It is found in coral reefs and coastal waters of the tropical Indo-Pacific. It grows to about three and a half inches in length from head to tail.

This little fish is scrappy and aggressive. It should be included only with other fishes physically and temperamentally able to cope with it. It is hardy and has been kept for several years in an aquarium.

It is shipped regularly to this country and arrives in splendid condition. We do not have a record of a spawning but it is one of the species that might very well be bred in the home aquarium.

It accepts brine shrimp, tiny pieces of raw shrimp and beef; lettuce should be offered if algae are absent from the aquarium. The aquarium in which this little fish is maintained should be furnished with coral or shells that offer hiding places.

Blue Demoiselle

The blue demoiselle (*Abudefduf caeruleus*, referred to as *Abudefduf saphirus* by Jordan and Richardson in *Fishes from Islands of the Philippine Archipelago*, 1906) is an oval, somewhat compressed fish with a rounded snout and a slightly concave caudal fin. Dealers sometimes

Helen Simkatis

Figure 48. BLUE DEMOISELLE (*Abudefduf caeruleus*)

mention this little fish on their lists as the blue devil, a name that we think is unduly sensational and entirely unfortunate. It is brilliant blue on the body with a black line from the top of the gill opening running through the eye to the snout. Another line curves up from the lower lip to the outer rim of the eye. Two narrow broken black lines occur on the cheek. One or sometimes two black spots appear on the peduncle just below the posterior dorsal. The dorsal, pectoral, ventral and anal fins are lightish and if examined closely prove to be a washed-out brown.

These little fishes come to us from the tropical Pacific coastal waters. They are said to reach three inches in length but the ones we receive seldom measure over an inch and a half in length.

The blue demoiselles are extremely colorful in the aquarium, their bright blue flashing beautifully as they dart in and out of holes in the coral. They are apt to be quite bossy when a new fish is introduced into an established aquarium. If the fish is larger than they, the problem is not so acute. It is far better for the new fish to be introduced into another aquarium where specimens of the blue demoiselles are not present. They are no match for the *Dascyllus trimaculatus* or *aruanus,* however, and should not be kept with either of these varieties unless they have been in the aquarium a long time and the newcomer is smaller. Even then the situation should be watched rather carefully, for although varieties of the *Dascyllus* seem to tolerate the clownfishes, they will not usually take kindly to the blue demoiselle.

This little fish compares with the clowns and *Dascyllus* for hardiness. It adjusts very well to aquarium conditions and can withstand the copper sulfate treatment given in the chapter on disease. When attacked by parasites, it bounces violently off rough surfaces and, should this condition exist, treatment should be given immediately.

They relish brine shrimp, tiny pieces of raw lean beef, and washed raw shrimp. They like lettuce and it should be included in their diet unless there is a healthy growth of algae present on the walls of the aquarium and on the coral.

As the blue demoiselle likes to swim in and out of holes in the coral and usually stakes out a claim in one section of the aquarium, such hiding places should be provided for it. It makes a peculiar little barking sound at any intruder that happens to swim near its chosen area. This usually happens at dusk when it is settling down for the night. We hear this sound when a clownfish invades the blue demoiselle's territory and its resemblance to a dog's bark is both striking and amusing.

With a little thought as to the temperament of this fish, you will find that it will add much to the aquarium by way of color and interest. It follows the clowns very closely in popularity among saltwater aquarists.

Heniochus Acuminatus

The *Heniochus acuminatus* (Linnaeus) does not have a vernacular or common name, although for hasty identification it is sometimes referred to as the pennant coralfish or bannerfish. It has not been

Helen Simkatis

Figure 49. *HENIOCHUS ACUMINATUS*

available to aquarists very long, but in a short period it has become very well liked by the hobbyists who have been fortunate enough to acquire it.

It is a compressed, deep fish, the fourth dorsal spine and attached membrane extending into a long, banner like appendage. The basic color is pearly white with two broad, black to purplish bands on the body. One originates at the first three spines of the dorsal and extends down through the pectoral to the ventral, and just touches the anal fin; it broadens as it approaches the underside of the fish. The other band originates just behind the long dorsal spine and extends to the tip of the anal fin, broadening as it reaches the undersides of the fish. A dusty black to purplish mask-like marking saddles the somewhat protruding snout and includes the eyes. This marking which bridges the snout gives the fish the appearance of having a turned-up nose. The soft portions of the dorsal, caudal, and pectoral fins are yellow. The adults are said to attain ten inches in length. This species is found in the coastal waters of the tropical Indo-Pacific.

It adapts very quickly to aquarium conditions and is without a doubt the most gentle fish we have ever encountered. It may be kept with considerably smaller specimens and the aquarist may be sure it will remain polite despite this advantage. It is very friendly and intelligent and within hours after being introduced into an aquarium, it will come up to the surface of the water and take food from the fingers. Although it seems to hold its own with such marauders as the *Dascyllus trimaculatus* and *aruanus,* it is better to keep this mannerly fish in gentler company.

It is priced rather high at the present time, but its hardiness and adaptability insure the risk. As its popularity increases, we hope that its price will decrease, as has been the case with other species that have become favorites.

Small pieces of beef and shrimp are received graciously and although our specimen is all of three and a half inches from head to tail, it relishes brine shrimp. An occasional feeding of adult brine shrimp should be offered. Lettuce should supplement the diet unless algae are present in the aquarium. As this species has a vigorous appetite, it should be fed at least twice a day. If the aquarist listens carefully when feeding it, he will hear distinct clicking sounds which apparently emanate from the mouth.

The *Heniochus acuminatus* shows no ill effects after having been given the copper sulfate treatment. Like all tropical marine fishes, however, it should not be exposed to chemically distorted water.

To summarize briefly on this species we might say this is one of the most ideal of the marine aquarium fishes. It has not gained the importance in the salt-water hobby as has the *Amphiprion percula* or the *Dascyllus aruanus* among marine aquarists simply because it is not as well known. Because this fish is unusually striking, along with being gentle and adaptable, there is no doubt it will become in the future one of the most important marine aquarium fishes.

Moorish Idol

The Moorish idol (*Zanclus cornutus*, Linnaeus) is a spectacular fish that has often been depicted in modern design because its interesting

Figure 50. MOORISH IDOL (*Zanclus cornutus*, Linnaeus)

and unusual lines lend themselves especially well to this medium. The first dorsal spine is short, as is the second, but the third is up to twice the total length of the fish in the young, growing somewhat shorter with age. The body is deep and compressed. The mouth is small and protruding. A hornlike growth appears above the eyes, which increases in size as the fish matures. The basic color is yellow with two broad, black to brown vertical bands present on the body. The anterior originates at the first dorsal spine and sweeps down the side of the fish, including the eyes and ventral fins. The second begins on the posterior dorsal ad continues down the sides of the fish to the anal fin. Both bands tend to broaden as they approach the undersides, and narrow blue vertical stripes are superimposed on them. A dark saddle is present on the somewhat elongated snout. The caudal fin is dark with a yellow border and a narrow stripe of blue separates the yellow from the dark section. Adults measure approximately nine inches in length.

The Moorish idol is widespread throughout the coastal waters of the Indo-Pacific and is found in reefs of shallow waters. It is shipped to this country from time to time but is priced beyond the means of most aquarists. Public aquariums, however, have displayed it rather frequently.

It has been kept in a closed-system aquarium for approximately three months. After this period, one aquarist reports, all three specimens present died suddenly. This would appear to be the result of a sudden drastic change rather than a food deficiency or a slow chemical change.

The aquarist who acquires specimens of this species, which is described by J. L. B. Smith as being a "lovely, rather pompous little fish," might add adult brine shrimp to the prescribed diet of small pieces of lean beef and raw shrimp. Lettuce should be offered if algae are not present in the aquarium.

Lionfishes

The lionfishes, as they are popularly called, are probably the most bizarre fishes ever kept in private aquariums. There are three varieties that commonly appear on dealers' lists and as they have much in common as to requirements and temperament, these aspects will not be treated separately.

The *Pterois volitans* is probably the best known of the three, and its long dorsal spines and pectoral rays give it the appearance of a strange bird in slow flight as it swims about the aquarium. It has a tentacle over the eye, the nape is scaleless, and the interorbital space

James Yates

Figure 51. LIONFISH (*Pterois volitans*)

is deeply concave. The orbital tentacles are said to become less conspicuous as the specimen grows older. The dorsal spines are one and a half times as long as the depth of the body and, although membrane is present on each, connective membrane is present only at the base. The body is reddish with vertical darker bands which are narrowly bordered with off-white. The basic reddish color sometimes darkens to almost black. Stripes differing in width and spacing radiate from the eyes. Ventral and anal fins are long and sweeping. The ventral spines are separate but covered with membrane flaps. Connective membrane is only present at the base. There are brown spots arranged in rows on the ventral, pectoral, soft dorsal and caudal fins. Adults reach about thirteen inches in length.

This fish occurs in tropical coastal Indo-Pacific waters and sometimes is found in estuaries. The very young are somewhat transparent and as the fish advances in age the colors become more pronounced. The spines are poisonous.

Another lionfish, *Pterois radiata* (Cuvier), is basically brown to black with lighter bands edged with off-white. The dorsal spines are long with membrane present but connective membrane is present only at the base. The pectoral spines are not separated and concentric lines are present. The interorbital space is concave and submarginate stripes radiate from the eyes. The basic color of the head is pinkish brown. It attains six inches in length.

The smallest of the lionfishes comes to us from Hawaii, *Dendrochirus chloreus* (Jenkins), although similar species are found in the coastal waters of the tropical Indo-Pacific. Dealers usually list it as the dwarf lionfish. It has long dorsal spines with connective membrane deeply cleft. The pectoral fins are round and the connective membrane is somewhat cleft and just misses reaching the caudal base. The ventral fins are long and full, and the caudal is slightly rounded. There is a vertical green band on the head beginning below the eye. Six yellow-green vertical bands appear on the body which is basically brown. The spinous dorsal is yellow-green with red spots; the soft dorsal has oblique bands of red and white. The anal fin has two olive bands followed by faded red and white stripes. It is said not to exceed four inches in length.

The lionfishes have proved to be successful in the closed-system aquarium and, despite the fact that each of the varieties we have mentioned must be handled with care because of their poisonous spines, they have become very popular among aquarists. Their weird beauty fascinates the hobbyist who seeks out the unusual and certainly there was never a better conversation piece.

One or two may be kept in an aquarium but care must be taken that a large one (at least thirty-five gallon) is used to accommodate them. They are not aggressive and we have seen another entirely different variety of fish (comparable in size) quite at ease in an aquarium containing several. This is not advisable, however, and it is not wise to keep more than two specimens in an aquarium as these fishes give off a slimy skinlike material, an accumulation of which would foul the water.

They will accept only live food. Guppies and small mollies are usually offered. The aquarist who dislikes feeding his pet live fishes had better forgo acquiring any of the lionfishes.

Braz Walker, an aquarist living in Waco, Texas, has written us about his specimens which he has had for over two years, one of which is shown in Figure 50. This fish is in artificial salts (Neptune) and has been kept in a thirty-gallon metal frame aquarium made by a manufacturer who recommends his tanks for salt-water use. In a little less than a year, this fish grew from slightly over five inches in length to eight. Mr. Walker attributes his success in maintaining this fish over such a substantial length of time to the power filter he uses which is run automatically from an electric timer. The pump (all the parts that come in contact with the aquarium water are made of plastic) runs intermittently, on an hour and off an hour, all around the clock. It is an inside, current-producing filter pump. The slimy, skinlike material which the fish occasionally sheds is picked up by the filter pump and is not allowed to accumulate in the water.

Any one of the lionfishes is spectacularly beautiful. They soon become quite tame and because of their striking colors and weird design, they are often kept solely for exhibition purposes in aquarium stores. They have proved to be hardy, as Mr. Walker's experience with his specimen indicates, and this makes them a good risk despite the fact they are quite expensive.

Suggested Reading

Walter H. Chute, *Guide to the John G. Shedd Aquarium*, 1953.

Oliver P. Jenkins, *Report on Collections of Fishes Made in the Hawaiian Islands with Descriptions of New Species*, U. S. Government Printing Office, 1903.

David Starr Jordan and Barton Warren Evermann, *Descriptions of New Genera and Species of Fishes from the Hawaiian Islands*, U. S. Government Printing Office, 1903.

David Starr Jordan and Robert Earl Richardson, *Fishes from Islands of the Philippine Archipelago*, 1908.

David Starr Jordan and Alvin Seale, *The Fishes of Samoa*, U. S. Government Printing Office, 1906.

Ian S. R. Munro, *The Marine and Fresh Water Fishes of Ceylon*, Department of External Affairs, Canberra, 1955.

Leonard P. Schultz and Collaborators: Earl S. Herald, Ernest A. Lachner, Arthur D. Welander and Loren P. Woods, *Fishes of the*

Marshall and Marianas Islands, Vol. 1, Smithsonian Institution, U. S. Government Printing Office, 1953.

J. L. B. Smith, *The Sea Fishes of Southern Africa,* Central News Agency, Ltd., South Africa, 1949.

CHAPTER 9

Estuary Fishes

Introduction to Estuary Fishes

MOST fishes taken from estuaries are hardy. All the fishes discussed in this chapter are found in estuaries and bays and, on a whole, they are easier to maintain than the salt-water tropicals. Their less specialized requirements give them enough in common to be included in one group although some may be collected by the hobbyist in his local coastal areas while others are shipped from the distant shores of Ceylon and other remote waters.

The harbors and estuaries of the world, infiltrated by industrial and human waste materials, have been the spawning grounds of these interesting fishes. They thrive under conditions that would be lethal to other types of marine animals because they enjoy wide tolerance to both chemical and biological changes. Some have journeyed far up into rivers and streams where the water is only slightly brackish and have prospered, adjusting to what would seem to be a completely unfavorable environment. This probably accounts for their ability to flourish in standard aquariums. The chemical changes that occur in the aquarium water as a result of its contacting standard aquarium cement does not seem to harm these hardy specimens. Many of them can be converted to fresh water entirely and all of them do very well in water of low salinity. Aeration is necessary and good housekeeping should be maintained, but if these requirements, along with regular feedings and usual care are provided, the aquarist can be relatively assured of a successful tank.

We haven't attempted to name all the likely candidates for this phase of the hobby and have confined ourselves to the popular species of fishes that fall into this category.

Unfortunately, we cannot advise those who are uninitiated in the salt-water hobby to begin with the estuary fishes as a first step toward becoming salt-water aquarists. The novice might just as well start with fresh-water specimens as neither these nor the estuary fishes are as fastidious in their requirements as are the reef fishes. We might, however, recommend the estuary fishes to the aquarist who doesn't wish to meet the challenge the reef fishes offer and yet would like to participate in a phase of the salt-water hobby, however less specialized.

In many instances the estuary fishes are colorful and attractive; in all instances they are interesting. Many of them can be collected by the aquarist and such a quest will offer added interest to a vacation spent at the seashore. Although we have stressed the hardiness of these fishes, we suggest that Chapter 5 of this book on collecting be reviewed carefully before starting out on such an adventure to assure the specimens' reaching the home aquarium in good condition. Aeration must be supplied during the journey home and suitable containers must be used.

The water they have been collected in may be used and, although a salinity reading should be taken at this time, the aquarist may gradually increase or decrease the degree of density as time goes by, according to his particular scheme. Water that is needed for future use may be a salt concentrate diluted to whatever salinity the aquarist has decided upon, or a synthetic mix may be used diluted, of course, in the same way. Even a good grade of aquarium salt can be used if only estuary fishes are to be included in the aquarium and the degree of salinity is to be kept down to a minimum.

If any of the estuary fishes are to be kept with fishes that require a high salinity (1.020 to 1.023), they should be conditioned to this degree of salinity in gradual steps and, of course, the requirements and standards necessary to maintain salt-water fishes will have to be followed.

There are many varieties within families of the estuary fishes but we have only listed a single type within a genus. To identify other types, we suggest that the books recommended for further reading which are listed at the end of this chapter be consulted.

ATLANTIC ESTUARY FISHES

Northern Puffer

The northern puffer (*Spheroides maculatus,* Bloch and Schneider) is a representative of a large genus of fishes which are frequently referred to as the swellfishes. We have chosen the northern puffer for discussion here because it is often collected by aquarists in estuaries and coastal waters along the Atlantic coast as far north as New York and at least as far south as the eastern shore of Maryland. Occasionally it is found as far north as Maine, but its occurrence there is rather uncommon.

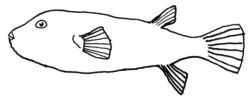

Figure 52. NORTHERN PUFFER (*Spheroides maculatus,* Bloch and Schneider)

The northern puffer, like the other members of its group, can take in air or water, which ever element is present, and inflate until it takes on a ball-like appearance. This defense mechanism is quite an efficient one as is evidenced by the success of the *Spheroides* as a group. When a sea gull swoops down into the water and catches one of these fishes, its victim immediately takes in air through its specialized breathing valves and becomes ball-shaped. Its scales become small prickles that stand out and this adds to the difficulty the bird experiences in trying to keep its prize. As a result, the fish is usually dropped back into the water to resume its normal existence. When a larger fish attacks the puffer, it depends on the same method of defense but in this case water is used for inflation.

The northern puffer is able to dig down into the sand by means of specialized clavicles under the loose ventral skin; these are used like shovels or as landing gear when the fish chooses to settle on the ocean floor. It is an elongated, odd-shaped fish, its eyes, which are set far apart, and small mouth give it a humorous face, especially in the young. The ventral fins are missing and the caudal fin is slightly rounded. The body is mottled green on the upper portion and pales out to an off-white on the ventral side. The dorsal fin occurs just before the base of the caudal peduncle and the anal is just a bit further back where the caudal and body meet. The northern puffer attains about ten inches in length.

These fishes seem to be a natural host for the parasite *Oödinium* and care should be taken that a specimen is free from this pest before allowing it to mingle with other fishes. As this fish shows no reaction from the copper sulfate treatment, it might be a good idea to administer this drug during the isolation period as a prophylactic measure.

The northern puffers can live in water of low salinity and have been kept successfully in standard aquariums. They are hearty eaters and relish small pieces of lean raw beef and raw shrimp. After they have partaken of such fare, their stomachs bulge unevenly, giving them a comical appearance. They like brine shrimp, too, and lettuce or algae should be included in their diet. They thrive very well in the aquarium and will not attack tankmates. They are active and startle rather easily. We have heard them jump out of the water and hit against the cover of their tank at night when we have gone into the room in which they are kept without turning on the light. It is not necessary to keep a heater in the aquarium.

Specimens measuring about an inch from head to tail will double their length within a year. Although they do not seem to be unhappy in the aquarium, they swim up and down the sides rather constantly disturbing other well-adjusted specimens. Because of this mannerism, we cannot class them as highly satisfactory aquarium specimens. They should not be kept as mere conversation pieces to be removed from their tank to swell up into a small ball for company. The entertainment value of such an exhibition is questionable and the fish may be damaged in the handling. They do make interesting specimens, however, and might be kept until they outgrow their quarters. We have

kept them for a little over two years and then released them in the
summer when the water was warm and conditions generally good for
their readjustment to natural conditions.

Northern Pipefish

The pipefishes belong to the same family as the sea horses and are
more or less covered with bony plates. The axis of the head is in line
with that of the body. The tail is non-prehensile, and the caudal fin
is evident. The gill holes are small and the gills are rounded tufts.
These fishes follow the reproduction method of the seahorses, the female inserting her ovipositor into the brood pouch on the abdomen

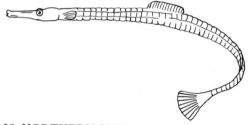

Figure 53. NORTHERN PIPEFISH (*Syngnathus fuscus,* Storer)

of the male where she deposits her eggs. Here the eggs are fertilized
and incubated. The young remain in the pouch until they are able
to fend for themselves, at which time they are expelled.

We have chosen the northern pipefish (*Syngnathus fuscus,* Storer) for
discussion here because it is the species usually found by collectors in
the tangled masses of seaweed found on the floors of inlets, estuaries
and bays along the coast from Halifax, Nova Scotia, to North Carolina. It is mottled green to brown and the depth of the body is equal
to the length of the head. It is said to reach twelve inches in length
although we have never found a specimen that measured over six
inches.

The northern pipefish is often found in estuaries of low salinity but
to our knowledge it has never been converted to strictly fresh water.
It does do well in brackish water, however, and can be kept with
other specimens that do well in water of low salinity. This fish adapts

well to aquarium conditions and accepts brine shrimp and daphnia readily. It is an avid eater and when it has become completely adjusted to life in captivity, it can be induced to accept small pieces of raw shrimp and beef. Like the sea horse, however, live food is definitely preferred. It has been maintained in standard aquariums and as it is not a tropical fish, no heater is required. Because it is extremely active, the slow-moving sea horse cannot compete with it at feeding time. It is not advisable to keep these species together as the sea horse seems to tire of trying to participate in this hopeless contest and becomes entirely apathetic to the business of eating.

Collecting the pipefish does not call for much skill on the part of the aquarist. Thrusting a hand net under a clump of seaweed in an area where the water is shallow and surfless usually pays off in several specimens. The rule of taking only a few fishes applies here, too, however, for should the aquarist take more than his containers can support, all of his specimens will die during the journey home.

Killifishes

The killifishes are old favorites among aquarists who have taken their hobby with them to the seashore during their summer vacations. Usually they have collected one variety or another of these little fishes and brought them back to their homes to be included among their aquarium pets. We have chosen the broad killifish (*Cyprinodon variegatus,* Lacépède) for discussion because we happen to know it better than the other species and have enjoyed this pleasant little fish both in our own aquariums and in those of our friends.

There are many species of killifishes and for their identification, we suggest that the hobbyist consult the books listed at the end of this chapter as suggested reading.

The broad killifish is oval and somewhat elongated. The posterior is more compressed than the anterior. During the breeding season (spring and early summer) the males are slate blue above and orange below. The females are black and off-white, the bodies marked with irregular vertical stripes. The stripes are present on the male also but are less vivid. These little fishes never reach more than three inches in length and are mature when about a year old. The females are

Figure 54. BROAD KILLIFISHES (*Cyprinodon variegatus,* Lacépède)

slightly smaller than the males. They are found in the shallows of bays and estuaries along the Atlantic coast and Gulf of Mexico from Cape Cod to Texas, in waters of low salinity. They can be converted to fresh water but some salinity is preferable.

They settle down to aquarium conditions rather soon after capture and they are a more or less uncomplicated species to care for. They have fared very well in standard aquariums. Brine shrimp, small pieces of raw beef and shrimp are accepted readily and lettuce should be included in the diet if a growth of algae is not present on the walls of the aquarium. They will take dry food, and relish chopped earthworms.

They spawn readily in the aquarium. The small eggs are globular and yellowish. They attach themselves to plant leaves, glass, or the bottom of the tank by thin threads. The spawning goes on for several days, a portion of the spawn being laid each day. The babies have been raised in the aquarium when freshly hatched brine shrimp and very fine dry food have been supplied.

The killifishes are easily caught by seining in shallow areas. Two people, one on either end of a small seine, wading knee-deep, can catch many specimens. The rule of taking only as many fishes as can be supported applies here, too.

The killifishes are successful aquarium pets because they adjust well to the aquarium community. They are not scrappy and the fact that they will spawn in the aquarium adds to their interest. No heater is necessary in their tank as they are not tropical fishes.

Two-Spined Stickleback

The two-spined stickleback (*Gasterosteus aculeatus,* Linnaeus) is well known among aquarists who collect specimens in the shallow inlets and estuaries along the Atlantic coast. Variations occur within this species, depending apparently on the salinity of the water in which individuals are found. Specimens collected in fresh or brackish water do not have the bony plates, nor is the structure of the dorsal spines and caudal keel as well developed as those of specimens found in marine water.

The two-spined stickleback is a slender, spindle-shaped fish with two anterior isolated dorsal spines; the first occurs above the pectoral base and the second above the ventrals. There is a soft posterior dorsal and the caudal peduncle is narrow. The caudal is slightly concave, and a ventral spine is present. Although these fishes are mature when two inches in length, they reach approximately four inches from head to tail.

During the spawning season (spring and early summer) the usually slate-colored male becomes blue above and somewhat rosy-hued ventrally. The interesting breeding habits of these little fishes have been the subject of numerous motion pictures and because they spawn readily in the aquarium they have become very popular among aquarists. The male builds a nestlike structure of bits of debris and vegetation over a depression he has made in the sand. The material of the nest is cemented together by an excretion from the kidneys. He anchors it over the depression by heaping sand over projecting pieces of the nesting material. He then tunnels through the cemented mass, forming a tubular structure. He is now ready for a partner and he actively courts any female stickleback that happens along. There is little finesse in his approach and he usually speeds matters up by driving the female into the tunnel of love he has fashioned. Here she lays her eggs which he vigorously and unceremoniously fertilizes. Then, with his inimitable lack of tact, he drives the female away. Several females may be courted in this roughshod manner until the tunnel is sufficiently lined with eggs. During the incubation, the male takes on his duty as guard over his potential progeny as energetically as he performed his chores of courtship. He fans the eggs and watches for marauders. It is best to remove the female from the aquarium at

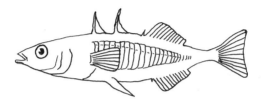

Figure 55. TWO-SPINED STICKLEBACK (*Gasterosteus aculeatus*, Linnaeus)

this point for she now appears to him as an enemy, and is dealt with as such. The incubation is completed in approximately ten days, depending on the prevailing temperature. The little father assumes responsibility for the fry until they are free-swimming. Be sure to supply enough brine shrimp for all parties, as father isn't above taking the lion's share.

Brine shrimp, small pieces of raw beef and shrimp, and dry food make a balanced diet for the stickleback. Lettuce should be offered if a growth of algae is not present on the walls of the aquarium.

The stickleback is collected by thrusting a hand net under clumps of seaweed. When the net is brought to the surface, each tangled piece of vegetation is rinsed within the frame of the net and discarded. Usually one or two specimens will be found at the bottom of the net.

If the males are found to be in breeding colors, it is a good idea to take only one. Two or three females can be included in the catch but two males will spell trouble.

As the stickleback is not a tropical fish, no heater is required in the aquarium. Temperatures over 70° Fahrenheit might not be tolerated. These little fishes settle down to aquarium life rather well and they need not be kept alone unless they show indications of spawning. During this period, the males will be quarrelsome not only with their own kind but with other species of fishes as well. Although they can be converted to entirely fresh water, some salinity is preferable.

The sticklebacks have been maintained successfully in standard aquariums; because of their interesting habits, their willingness to spawn in captivity and the simplicity of their maintenance, they make fine aquarium pets.

Sail-Fin Molly

The sail-fin molly (*Mollienesia latipinna,* Lesueur) is in reality a brackish-water fish and often is found in sea water, but fresh-water aquarists have claimed and converted this little fish to their medium for so long and so completely that the fact that it originates in water of both high and low salinity has almost been forgotten.

Its origin became more obscure when its melanistic tendency was picked up and sustained in what is now an all-time favorite known as the black sail-fin molly, a pure black fish and one of the most important fishes in the fresh-water hobby.

Despite the fact that the black sail-fin molly is one of the most popular fresh-water fishes and that beginners often start with a "gravid female" in order that their newly acquired aquarium pet might have her offspring in their tank, it has been consistently one of the most difficult fishes to maintain in a healthy condition for its natural life span. We feel that this is partly due to the fact that the molly does better in brackish water and our opinion is backed by the fact that the healthiest mollies we have raised were bred and born in water with a salinity equal to that in which we have maintained our marine tropicals.

The sail-fin molly is an elongated fish, the male of the species having a showy dorsal fin which often runs the length of the body or from just behind the nape to the beginning of the caudal base, and stands as high as the width of the body. The basic color is a silvery olive and dots appear along the sides. The female is considerably

Figure 56. SAIL-FIN MOLLY (*Mollienisia latipinna,* Le Sueur)

This black molly has been reconverted to salt water. (Note anemone which cannot live in fresh water.)

larger than the male and her dorsal fin is not as high, nor does it extend to the base of the caudal. These fishes sometimes attain a length of three and a half inches but two and a half to three is usual.

The mollies are livebearers, the females expelling from thirteen to twenty youngsters about every thirty days, when once impregnated, for a period that may last as long as a year. The babies are born large enough to take freshly hatched brine shrimp and prepared dried food especially designed for newborn fishes.

It is far better to have several females to one male as when only one female is present in the aquarium, the male becomes overly persistent in his attentions to her, and the harassed female has little time to find food or rest.

The sail-fin mollies are never quarrelsome toward other fishes or among themselves and make ideal members of an aquarium community. They should not be crowded, however, and should be kept by themselves if the fry are to be reared.

Mollies like brine shrimp, prepared dry food, daphnia, and if a growth of algae is not present on the walls of the aquarium, lettuce and spinach should be offered. Vegetation is important in their diet.

These fishes can be purchased from most dealers as a fresh-water fish. If the aquarist wishes to convert his specimens to brackish or sea water, he should do so gradually, taking at least a week to complete the change. No fish should be converted to salt water abruptly; although some species might survive the change, it could be fatal to others.

The aquarist who likes to collect his own specimens will find the sail-fin molly in estuaries, inlets, and bays along the Atlantic coast from the Carolinas to the Gulf of Mexico. A small seine is an ideal piece of equipment for such a venture.

EXOTIC ESTUARY FISHES

Scat   *Monodactylus*

Archerfish

Scat

There are several species of scats, all of which are desirable aquarium fishes, especially suited for the brackish-water medium. *Scatophagus argus* (Linnaeus) is by far the most popular member of the Scatophagidae in this country and because of this we have chosen it for discussion here. It has been shipped here indirectly from Ceylon for a number of years and as it converts readily to fresh water, it has become an important import for the fresh-water market. It is found in estuaries, however, and does exceedingly well in water of low salinity, which makes it ideal for those aquarists who wish to maintain brackish-water aquariums.

Scatophagus argus (Linnaeus) is a compressed, deep, and rather sturdy fish. The nape ascends sharply to the snout, giving it an unusual profile. The basic color is greenish gray to brown, although in another

John Hoke

Figure 57. THE SCAT (*Scatophagus argus,* Linnaeus)

color phase the basic color is reddish.[1] Many dark brown spots are superimposed on the basic color and are sometimes sprinkled lightly on the anterior dorsal. The undersides are silvery and the fins are pink to brownish gray. There are no structural differences between the basically green and the basically red scats and they are considered to be of the same species.

These fishes are found in quiet waters off Ceylon, some in the estuaries that contain water of low salinity, and others in sea water. They are shipped regularly to this country and arrive in the good condition that has come to be expected of shipments from this source. They adapt well to aquarium conditions and have been kept for several years in standard aquariums. If the aquarist desires to reconvert them

[1] Rodney Jonklaas of the Vavasseur Trading Company in Colombo, Ceylon, gives a very fine account of these fishes in his article entitled, "Concerning Scats," in the August, 1956, issue of *The Aquarium.*

to water of low salinity, the change should be made gradually. Although it may do well in fresh water, the scat does better in brackish water.

It is a scrappy fish and often will give more docile specimens considerable trouble. As it takes on size, it becomes showy and very attractive. Its bright coloring could well warrant its being kept in an aquarium by itself or with another of its own kind. Two often quarrel but couples have been known to get along rather well together.

Feeding poses no problem with this species. Small pieces of raw beef and shrimp are accepted readily and dry food may be offered as a supplement. Earthworms are relished and daphnia and brine shrimp are never refused. Duckweed should be present in the aquarium. These fishes must have vegetable matter and if duckweed is not available, the aquarist should try other types of greenery such as lettuce or cabbage until he hits on the one preferred.

Adults run to twelve inches in length in the wild state, although a pair measuring six inches from snout to tail is reported to have spawned in an aquarium. As these fishes take on size, the dorsal spines become poisonous. A hand or arm pierced by one of these will be painful for several hours.

Monodactylus

THE *Monodactylus argenteus* (Linnaeus) is usually referred to by aquarists by its generic name. It is a deep, compressed fish, the nape ascending sharply to the snout, making the high dorsal fin seem even higher. The anal fin is long and proportionate to the dorsal, giving this already deep fish an exaggerated depth. The brilliant silvery coloring is broken by two vertical stripes, one of which passes through the eye and the other from behind the nape through the pectoral base to the abdomen. These appear only on the young and fade out as the fish matures.

This fish is found in estuaries and will enter fresh water. It is widespread in the coastal waters of the tropical Indo-Pacific. Here another species is found also, the *Monodactylus falciformis,* which is shaped much the same as the *argenteus* but the silvery coloration is irridescent and no vertical stripes appear on the young.

Both the *argenteus* and *falciformis* do very well in the aquarium with water of low salinity. They are peaceful and are not able to withstand the attacks of an aggressor. These fishes are shipped regularly into this country and although usually presented to fresh-water aquarists, they are especially suited for the brackish-water aquarium where they fare better than in strictly fresh water.

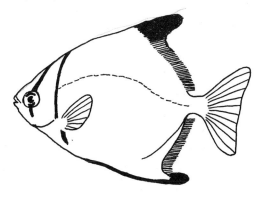

Figure 58. *MONODACTYLUS ARGENTEUS* (Linnaeus)

Small pieces of raw shrimp and beef are accepted and brine shrimp and daphnia are relished. Some lettuce should be offered if algae are not established in the aquarium.

Archerfish

The archerfish (*Toxotes chatareus,* Hamilton-Buchanan), like the little stickleback and sea horse, has been star of many a filmed short subject and owes this attention to the fact that, as its scientific and popular names suggest, it is a marksman of considerable ability. This fish can shoot down an insect that is some distance above the water by ejecting a series of drops of water from its highly specialized mouth and hitting its target with enough force to kill it. It is said that when the youngsters are only an inch long, they begin to develop their skill and by the time they are full-grown, their apprenticeship has been served, and they are sharpshooters in the fullest sense. Not only can they bring down an unsuspecting fly, meditating on a leaf, but insects in flight, as well. Aim is taken below the surface of the water, which means that allowance for refraction must be made.[1]

The archerfish is oblong and compressed. The head is flat and there is little or no ascent of the nape to the snout. The terminal mouth is wide and protractile. The basic color is silver with a yellowish tinge. The back is dark with black blotches. The fins are yellow and dark margins appear on the anal and dorsal. The eyes are unusually large.

The archerfish is found in the waters off Ceylon in brackish water of lagoons and estuaries. Another species (*Toxotes jaculator,* Pallas) is found in waters off India, Burma, Malaya, the Philippines, Indochina and Siam. (See Fig. 59.)

Figure 59. ARCHERFISH (*Toxotes jaculator,* Pallas)

The archerfish has been shipped to this country as a fresh-water specimen since it converts relatively easily. It can be included, however, in the aquarium set up for the brackish medium as it is at home in water of low salinity.

Small pieces of raw shrimp and beef will be accepted and brine shrimp and daphnia should be offered to specimens measuring from one to three inches. These fishes will feed on young guppies and mollies avidly but they do not necessarily require live food. They require at least two feedings a day. They will do very well in an aquarium equipped with a power filter, although constant standard aeration is adequate.

It is said to be peaceful among fishes comparable to it in size.

---

[1] There is an account of the remarkable mechanism of the oral cavity which enables the archerfish to shoot down its prey in the *Bulletin* of the U.S. Nat. Mus. 188, 490–497, 1945, by Hugh M. Smith. George S. Myers tells how the shooting apparatus of the archerfish was discovered in his article in the *Aquarium Journal,* October, 1952.

Suggested Reading

Percy Spencer Barnhart, *Marine Fishes of Southern California,* University of California Press, 1936.

William Beebe and John Tee-Van, *Field Book of the Shore Fishes of Bermuda,* Putnam, 1933.

Charles M. Breder, Jr., *Field Book of Marine Fishes of the Atlantic Coast,* Putnam, 1948.

CHAPTER 10

A Summary

The Established Aquarium Community · Ideal
Combinations of Fishes · A Final Word

The Established Aquarium Community

THE salt-water aquarium, once established, is comparatively simple to maintain, provided that no changes are made as to its general make-up other than the addition of fresh water to compensate for water lost due to evaporation.

An established aquarium community (*see* Figure 60) is one that has been set up for at least three months. The specimens it contains are adjusted to one another and are in good condition. Each member of the community has its place in the social pattern, successfully competes for food, acts alert, and its general behavior is normal. Some of the specimens will have stations, usually in holes in the coral or in shells, and will have no great difficulty in maintaining their territories. The specimens who do not take over such areas will have sleeping places where they rest at night without interference from tankmates. It usually takes from two to three months for the formation of such an orderly pattern.

Changes that are made in such an aquarium should be considered most carefully before execution; for the balance that has been established can easily be lost by the addition of new specimens or even by moving the aquarium to another location where there is a different amount of daylight. The addition of recently acquired coral or a complete change of water might affect the equilibrium of the established aquarium.

The sensitivity of the balance is due not only to the chemical nature of salt water and the metabolism of salt-water specimens, but also to

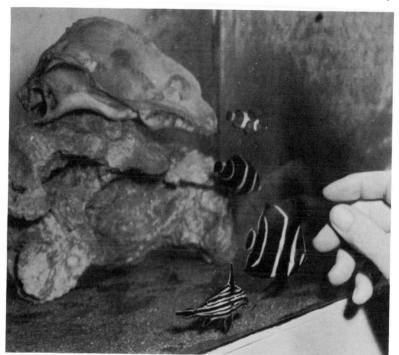

Helen Sinkatis

Figure 60. AN ESTABLISHED AQUARIUM COMMUNITY

the personality traits of the species that make up the population of the established community. Although some marine tropicals such as the French and black angels and any of the butterfly fishes do not, strictly speaking, claim territories, and as a result do not attack newcomers, most of the reef fishes do take over stations and guard them jealously; they will not, once established, tolerate the threat posed by newly introduced specimens. If the stranger is at all shy, it will be harassed and chased until it dies of sheer exhaustion or injuries sustained either through conflict with its tormentors or by dashing against coral or aquarium walls in its flight to escape them.

The personalities of fishes on hand should, therefore, be studied most carefully before introducing additional specimens. If the aquarium population is made up of *Dascyllus trimaculatus* or *aruanus,* blue demoiselles, Beau Gregories or, to a lesser degree, clowns or gobies, and such a group of fishes has been living in harmony for several months, new specimens should be delegated to another aquarium rather than being exposed to the rage of members of the established community. Even specimens that are able to withstand the onslaught of inhospitable tankmates live in fear and become neurotic, and often cannot compete for food or places of refuge in the coral. As a result, they languish and eventually die of malnutrition if they are not injured fatally at the time of their introduction.

The chemical upset in the water of an established community by the introduction of additional specimens is not so quickly discovered as is the disturbance in the social pattern. It can be just as detrimental to the well-being of the aquarium, however, and occurs when the aquarist tries to keep more fishes than the capacity of his tank can support. A good rule to follow to avoid making this mistake is to allow five gallons of water for every fish whether it measures an inch in length or three. For specimens measuring from three to four inches, ten gallons of water for each should be the rule. A specimen that measures over four inches and up to six should have at least twenty-five gallons of water. These specimens, however, are rather large for the home aquarium and would be far better omitted. Salt-water fishes cannot be crowded in the way that fresh-water fishes are, the rule applying to them being (though seldom observed) an inch of fish to a gallon of water. Because of the chemical nature of salt water, five gallons per fish from one to three inches in length is not a loose figure with a wide margin.

Under no conditions should a new specimen be introduced to the established aquarium community without being placed in an observation tank for at least ten days. Such an introduction is an open invitation to parasites and disease.

Moving the aquarium is sometimes necessary, but before its new location is chosen, the amount of daylight it will receive should be considered. A tank that has a well-established growth of algae on its walls due to exposure to sunlight should not be moved to a place where little or no sunlight will reach it. If such a move is made, the established algae growth dies from lack of sunlight and quantities of carbon diox-

ide have to be dealt with as well as the organic waste material resulting from the dead and dying vegetation. If such a move cannot be
avoided, the removal of the established crop of algae will be necessary.

The introduction of new coral or shells is the least harmful of the
possible changes we have mentioned. The elected coral should be
treated as recommended in the section on ornaments and decor in
Chapter 2 of this book.

Although a complete change of water is on the whole a beneficial
change, the aquarist is actually introducing a new chemical environment in which a kind of balance will eventually be attained. We do
not suggest that a perfect biogical equilibrium is ever present in an
aquarium. We use the term "balance" to describe the condition that
exists when aeration and photosynthesis are sufficient to keep the
water in such condition that it can support a limited number of specimens.

We have covered the most common changes that are made in the
established aquarium, but others that we have not mentioned might
be necessary. Before making any change in the tank, consider whether
or not it is necessary, whether it will affect the chemical balance of the
water, or if it will upset the social pattern of the established specimens.
It is interesting to note that whenever impressive longevity records
have been attained, changes of any kind have been held down to a
minimum.

Maintaining a log or aquarium diary is extremely helpful to the
aquarist. Such a record should contain the dates specimens have been
acquired, their respective sources, the manner of shipment employed,
a description of their condition when received, and so forth. The
changes that have been made should be noted, as well as the reasons
behind them. Patterns soon become apparent in such a log and, on
looking back, the aquarist is able to discover and correct mistakes he
may have made. A written record is far better than depending on
memory. It is surprising how many details can be forgotten unless
they have been carefully recorded at the time of their occurrence.
Many times our written records prove invaluable to us when we are
trying to pin down a cause for an unfavorable condition or an indication that all is not well in one of our aquariums.

Ideal Combinations of Fishes

The following combinations of marine tropical fishes have been found successful by salt-water hobbyists and are suggested as possible candidates for ideal aquarium communities.

As the size of the aquarium used determines the number of fishes desirable, we have based our suggestions on the sizes of aquariums usually available.

The Ten-gallon Aquarium[1]

No. 1.   2 dwarf sea horses and family of 10 babies

No. 2.   2 neon gobies

No. 3.   2 sea horses (*Hippocampus punctulatus* or *hudsonius*)

No. 4.   1 Jewel fish and 1 hermit crab

The Fifteen-gallon Aquarium

No. 1.   2 clownfishes (*A. percula* or *bicinctus*)

   1 hermit crab

No. 2.   2 *Dascyllus trimaculatus* or *aruanus*

   1 hermit crab

No. 3.   1 small black or French angel

   1 small butterfly fish (any one of them)

   1 hermit crab

No. 4.   1 Beau Gregory

   1 *Dascyllus trimaculatus* or *aruanus*

   1 hermit crab

No. 5.   1 small rock beauty (1 to 2 inches in length)

   1 hermit crab

---

[1] The ten-gallon tank is not recommended for salt-water fishes as its capacity is considered too small. These combinations are generally acceptable, however, but under no conditions should additional specimens be added.

No. 6.   1 queen or blue angel (1 to 2 inches in length)

         1 hermit crab

No. 7.   2 sergeant majors (1 to 2 inches in length)

         1 hermit crab

No. 8.   1 lionfish (*Dendrochirus chloreus*) (2 to 3 inches in length)

No. 9.   1 high hat (1 to 2 inches in length)

         1 French or black angel (1 to 2 inches)

No. 10.   2 neon gobies

         1 cowfish (1 inch to 2 inches in length)

No. 11.   1 spiny boxfish (1 to 2 inches in length)

         1 hermit crab

No. 12.   1 high hat (1 to 2 inches in length)

         1 cardinal (1 to 2 inches in length)

No. 13.   1 blue demoiselle

         2 clownfishes (*A. percula* or *bicinctus*)

No. 14.   2 butterfly fishes (any variety)

         1 high hat

The Twenty-five-gallon Aquarium

No. 1.   2 French or black angels
(2 specimens ascertained to be on friendly terms)

         2 butterfly fishes (any variety)

         1 hermit crab

No. 2.   2 clownfishes (*A. percula* or *A. bicinctus*)

         2 butterfly fishes (any variety)

         1 blue demoiselle

         1 hermit crab

No. 3.   2 clownfishes (any variety)

2 *Dascyllus trimaculatus* or *aruanus*

1 hermit crab

No. 4.   1 blue demoiselle

1 French or black angel (1 to 3 inches)

2 clownfishes (any variety)

1 hermit crab

No. 5.   2 high hats

1 hermit crab

2 neon gobies

No. 6.   1 cowfish (1 to 3 inches)

1 spiny boxfish (1 to 3 inches)

2 butterfly fishes (any variety)

1 hermit crab

No. 7.   1 Lionfish (*Pterois radiata* or *volitans* not more than 4 inches in length)

No. 8.   1 *Heniochus acuminatus*

2 butterfly fishes (any variety)

1 high hat

No. 9.   1 *Heniochus acuminatus* (2 to 3 inches)

2 neon gobies

1 hermit crab

No. 10.   1 French or black angel (1 to 3 inches)

2 clownfishes (any variety)

1 *Dascyllus trimaculatus* or *aruanus*

The Thirty-gallon Aquarium

No. 1.   1 *Heniochus acuminatus*

2 clownfishes (any variety)

2 high hats

1 hermit crab

No. 2. 2 clown fishes (any variety)

1 blue demoiselle

1 black or French angel (2 to 3 inches)

1 *Heniochus acuminatus* (introduce this fish before the French angel)

No. 3. 1 blue demoiselle (introduce this fish last)

2 clownfishes

1 butterfly fish (any variety)

1 black or French angel

No. 4. 2 neon gobies

2 clownfishes (any variety)

1 butterfly fish (any variety)

No. 5. 1 cowfish

1 spiny boxfish

2 butterfly fishes

1 *Heniochus acuminatus*

No. 6. 2 sergeant majors

1 Beau Gregory

1 *Dascyllus trimaculatus* or *aruanus*

1 French angel

No. 7. 2 *Heniochus acuminatus*

1 cardinal

1 French angel

The Thirty-five-Gallon Aquarium

No. 1. 2 butterfly fishes (any variety)

2 clownfishes (any variety)

1 blue demoiselle

1 French or black angel

No. 2.   2 high hats

1 rock beauty

1 butterfly fish (any variety)

2 neon gobies

No. 3.   2 sergeant majors

1 Beau Gregory

2 *Dascyllus trimaculatus* or *aruanus*

1 French or black angel

1 hermit crab

No. 4.   2 Moorish idols

1 hermit crab

No. 5.   1 queen angel

2 *Dascyllus trimaculatus* or *aruanus* (number of fishes in this combination reduced due to temperaments of species suggested)

No. 6.   1 jewel fish

2 *Dascyllus trimaculatus* or *aruanus*

1 blue angel
(number of fishes in this combination reduced due to temperaments of species suggested)

No. 7.   1 French or black angel

1 butterfly fish (any species)

2 high hats

2 cardinals

The Forty-gallon Aquarium

No. 1.   1 rock beauty (1 to 4 inches)

2 *Dascyllus trimaculatus* or *aruanus*

No. 2.   2 clownfishes (any variety)

1 rock beauty

2 neon gobies

2 butterfly fishes (any variety)

No. 3.   1 French or black angel

1 butterfly fish (any variety)

2 clownfishes (any variety)

1 cardinal

2 high hats

No. 4.   2 clownfishes (any variety)

2 butterfly fishes (any variety)

2 neon gobies

1 *Heniochus acuminatus*

No. 5.   2 moorish idols

1 hermit crab

2 neon gobies

No. 6.   1 French or black angel

2 butterfly fishes (four-eyed)

2 butterfly fishes (common)

2 *Heniochus acuminatus*

No. 7.   2 butterfly fishes (any variety)

1 high hat

2 neon gobies

2 clownfishes (any variety)

The Fifty-gallon Aquarium

No. 1.   2 sergeant majors

2 blue demoiselles

2 clownfishes (any variety)

2 high hats

1 French or black angel

1 hermit crab

No. 2. 2 cardinals

2 Clownfishes (*A. percula*)

1 *Heniochus acuminatus* (3 to 4 inches)

1 hermit crab

No. 3. 2 clownfishes *A. percula*

2 blue demoiselles (introduce last)

2 butterfly fishes (any variety)

1 high hat

2 French or black angels
(an established, friendly couple)

1 hermit crab

No. 4. 2 clownfishes (*A. percula*) ⎱ Introduced the
2 clownfishes (*A. bicinctus*) ⎰   same time

1 four-eyed butterfly

2 neon gobies

2 *Heniochus acuminatus*

No. 5. 2 cowfishes

2 spiny boxfishes (1 to 3 inches)

2 butterfly fishes (any variety)

2 high hats

1 French or black angel

If the number of species in a suggested combination are counted the reader will note that the total usually equals one specimen less than the given capacity of a tank warrants, when the rule one fish to five gallons of water is followed. This is because we have allowed five gallons of water for replacement by coral or shells. We did not suggest a hermit crab in all of the listed combinations, but a specimen of one of these little creatures is always a valuable asset in an aquarium. By all means add one to your aquarium community if you happen upon a specimen. One is sufficient, however. Five gallons of water should be allowed for a sea anemone and it is wise to settle for one that doesn't measure more than four inches across.

Suggested Combinations of Estuary Fishes for the Brackish-Water Aquarium

The Ten-gallon Aquarium

No. 1.   2 sticklebacks

No. 2.   2 killifishes

No. 3.   2 pipefishes

No. 4.   1 pipefish

         1 puffer

The Fifteen-gallon Aquarium

No. 1.   2 female sail-fin mollies

         1 male sail-fin molly

No. 2.   2 killifishes

         1 female sail-fin molly

No. 3.   2 scats (1 to 2 inches in length)

No. 4.   2 *Monodactylus*

No. 5.   1 pipefish

         1 puffer

         1 *Monodactylus*

No. 6.   2 puffers

1 scat (2 inches)

No. 7.   2 archerfishes

The Twenty-gallon Aquarium

No. 1.   2 killifishes

2 puffers

No. 2.   2 scats (3 inches)

No. 3.   2 *Monodactylus*

1 pipefish

No. 4.   2 female sail-fin mollies

1 male

(The population of this tank will increase—it will support three adults and approximately 10 to 15 babies. These should be transferred to another aquarium when they attain a half inch in length.)

A Final Word

We have put together the knowledge we have gleaned during the years we have been working with salt-water tropical fishes. Through a lengthy process of elimination, we have discarded theories acquired here and there along the way when they proved to be faulty under actual test. With admitted pride, we added new ones when they were successful. Considerable time has been spent in merely organizing the methods we found worthy in a way that they will be most accessible to the aquarist when seeking the answers to the many problems that arise when participating in the marine hobby. Our avocation is in its infancy. As it gains popularity, new theories and methods will be discovered. We eagerly look forward to these developments. Many gains can be made in our hobby by way of equipment designed especially for it, new formulas for sea water, and so forth. The handling of disease and parasites has barely been approached. As time goes by, however, and many minds become busy with these problems, they will be solved.

As in all catalogs of facts, personal experiences and pleasant incidents would have been out of place in our book, although sometimes we risked incongruity and included a few. We feel, however, that the reader will not be conscious, when reading the preceding pages, that most of the information resulted from what my husband and I consider was, and is, high adventure.

There was no place in the book to mention the chuckles we enjoyed when our favorite hermit crab pompously took over a shell that was far too large for him, and the persuasion and tact we had to exercise to get it away from him in order that he might climb into a more suitable garment. Nor was there an opportunity to mention the time that our electric pump failed while we were in transit from Islamorada, Florida, to Washington, D.C., and we used a bicycle pump to aerate the jugs that contained our specimens—a long push and pull to say the least. We have omitted the delights we knew as we sped over the sun-drenched, azure waters of the Florida Keys to a favorite collecting spot and the intoxication we felt the day we caught our first pair of four-eyed butterfly fishes. All of these pleasant memoirs would be out of place in a book of instruction. Yet, we should be happy if we could bring to our readers only a portion of the pleasure and sense of accomplishment our hobby has brought to us. For city people, such as we are, who live in the great gray cubes we call apartment houses, surrounded by gray concrete sidewalks on which we walk to offices that are appropriately decorated in varying shades of something just between black and white, our hobby has become the riot of color we miss in our achromatic environment. As we shop at the supermarket, run to the post office, or do any of the everyday things, we do them just a little more happily than we would if we didn't have within the four walls we call home, a tiny tropical reef which we have captured from the sea. We have caught something of the wonderful summers we have known and we shall keep it all through the inevitable winters.

We bring these thoughts to you simply because we have found something that is at once creative, colorful and, most of all, fun! We bring them to you because we want to share them.

All hobbies are good for the soul. We feel that our hobby is more than that, for through it we become more conscious that we have one. When I examine under my microscope a tiny scale from one of nature's many masterpieces, the four-eyed butterfly fish, and become aware of the design, color and craftsmanship that have gone into it, I feel a surge of pure wonder at the miracle of all living things and I'm humbly grateful that I, too, am part of it.

Our hobby has taken us many places without our ever having set foot on a train or ocean liner. It has introduced us to great writers and observers of nature and allowed us to share their thoughts without the formality of an invitation. Vicariously, we have explored the coastal waters of seas that before were only names on a map to us. And we have housed some of the living things of these foreign waters and are constantly enchanted by their charm and beauty. Through our hobby, we are on speaking terms with the mysterious loveliness of the sea. It has widened our understanding of the greatest design, and enlivened our appreciation for it, and because of our mint-bright interest, our time for living has new value. These are high-sounding words for a hobby, but because ours has meant all of these things to us, we invite you to share it with us.

GLOSSARY AND INDEX

GLOSSARY

Algae (*singular,* alga): Any plant of a group comprising practically all seaweeds, as rockweed, sea lettuce and others, and allied fresh-water or nonaquatic forms, having no roots; capable of photosynthesis, taking in nutrients from every part of plant rather than just roots.

Anal: Pertaining to or situated near the anus.

Anal fin: The unpaired fin on the median line of the body of most fishes, behind the anus or vent.

Anterior: Situated at or relatively nearer to the front or head end (usually the end directed forward when animal is moving).

Anthozoans: Sea anemones, corals, etc. Class of Coelenterata; polyp more complexly organized than that of other Coelenterata.

Arteries: Blood vessel carrying blood from the heart toward the tissues.

Brine shrimp (Artemia): A tiny crustacean that is used for food for aquarium fishes. It is hatched from an egg that will remain fertile for as long as two years if it is kept in a sealed container.

Capillary: Minute tube conveying blood which it receives from a small artery and gives it up to a small vein; with a wall consisting of a single layer of flattened cells (endothelium) supported by fine connective tissue fibers. The main exchange of substance between blood and tissues occurs through capillaries.

Carbohydrates: Compound of sugars, starch and cellulose, playing an essential part in metabolism of all organisms.

Carotene: Orange pigment (hydrocarbon) synthesized by green plants, present in chloroplasts, and in plastids in parts where chlorophyll is absent. Carotene of food is changed into vitamin A in vertebrate liver.

Caudal: Of, pertaining to, or like, a tail; situated in or near the tail or hind end of the body.

Caudal fin: The unpaired fin at the posterior end of body; the tail fin.

Caudal peduncle: The region of the body between the dorsal and anal fins and the caudal fin.

Chlorophyll: The green matter of plants, occurring in the chloroplasts of cells exposed to light. Chlorophyll is essential in the formation of carbohydrates by photosynthesis.

Chloroplasts: A plastid containing chlorophyll developed only in plant cells exposed to light. Chloroplasts are the seat of photosynthesis and starch formation.

Chondrichthyes: Cartilaginous fish characterized by absence of true bone (sharks, skates, dogfish, rays).

Chromatophore: Cell with pigment in its cytoplasm.

Clavicle: Membrane-bone of ventral side of shoulder girdle of many vertebrates. (Corresponds to collarbone of man.)

Closed-system aquarium: In this book this expression designates the aquarium that contains a given volume of water that is both aerated and filtered within the aquarium itself. This type of aquarium is used in the home. The designation *closed-system aquarium* is also used in reference to certain public aquariums that have a number of aquariums in a circulating system, drawing water from a main reservoir. Each tank receives water from a line running from the reservoir, and each tank discharges water into a line that conducts it to the filtering area. When it passes through the filter, it returns to the reservoir where once again it goes through the system.

Coelenterata: Phylum of animals containing hydroids, jellyfish, sea anemones, corals, comb-jellies. All aquatic, most marine. Body build on a fairly simple plan.

Compressed: Flattened from side to side.

Coral: The calcareous or hornlike skeleton of various anthozoans; also, the entire animal which produces this skeleton.

Corpuscle: A protoplasmic cell, especially one of those that float free in blood, lymph, and pus.

Cytoplasm: All the protoplasm of a cell, excluding the nucleus. It is usually a transparent, slightly viscous fluid with inclusions of various sizes ranging from microscopically visible plastids to invisible "small particles" (microsomes).

Density: The quantity of dissolved material in solution.

Depressed: Flattened from above to below.

Depth: The greatest vertical diameter of a fish.

Dermal: Describing innermost of the two layers of the skin of vertebrates, the outer being the epidermal skin. The dermal skin is much thicker than the epidermis and consists of connective tissue with abundant collagen fibers mainly parallel to surface; scattered cells, blood and lymph vessels, sensory nerves.

Dinoflagellates: An order of mostly marine flagellates (subclass phytomastigina), including the peridinians, having two flagellata in about the middle of the body. Most of these organisms are commonly treated by botanists as forming a class of plants while biologists differ as to classing them as plants or animals, as they have characteristics of both forms.

Dorsal: Pertaining to, or situated near or on the back, or dorsum, of an animal or one of its parts.

Dorsal fin: The unpaired median fin of the back.

Ecology: The study of the relations of animals and plants, particularly of animal and plant communities, to their surroundings, animate and inanimate.

Elasmobranchii: Cartilaginous fish. Synonymous with Chondrichthyes except the Holocephali, rare fishes of this class that differ from elasmobranchii in that they have gill plates or opercula.

Epoxies: A class or group of plastic materials, having certain characteristics in common.

Esophagus: Part of gut between pharynx and stomach, concerned with passing food along by peristalsis.

Flagellata (Mastigophora): Class of protozoa characterized by possession of one or more flagella. Includes both plant and animal-like forms and some with mixed characteristics.

Flagella (*singular,* flagellum): Fine long threads having sinuous movement, projecting from a cell. Means of locomotion of those unicellular organisms and reproducing cells which bear them.

Fusiform: Spindle-shaped or tapering at the ends.

Gills: Respiratory organs of aquatic animals.

Guanine: A base ($C_5H_5N_5O$) occurring in liver, pancreas, muscles, and in some plants. In fish, excreted by the pancreas and found in the scales, bladder, skin, and the silvery layer of the eye. It causes the iridescence of some fishes.

Hormone: Organic substance produced in minute quantity in some part of an organism and transported to other parts where it exerts a profound effect.

Hydrometer: A floating instrument for determining specific gravities, especially of liquids, and hence the strength of saline solutions, etc.

Hydrozoans: Of or pertaining to the class (Hydrozoa) of coelenterates which includes various simple and compound polyps and jellyfishes.

Ichthyology: Study of fish; the department of zoology that treats of fishes broken down into three divisions: (1) Identification and classification of species; (2) Economic importance of fishes in relation with the welfare of mankind; (3) Study of fishes and their place in the natural design of living things.

Interorbital: The region of the head between the eyes.

Keel: Imaginary line running horizontally in mid-section of peduncle.

Lateral line: System of sense organs present in aquatic vertebrates, in pores or canals arranged in a line along each side of the body and in complicated patterns on head.

Littoral: Of or pertaining to the shore—a coastal region.

Melanin: A dark pigment.

Metabolism: The sum of the processes concerned in the building up of protoplasm and its destruction (catabolism incidental to life). The chemical changes in living cells by which the energy is provided for the vital processes and activities, and new material is assimilated.

Nutrient: A nutritious substance. That which nourishes.

Ocellus: A little eye; an eyelike spot.

Operculum: Plate covering gill-slits of fish.

Orbicular: Resembling, or having the form of, an orb; circular.

Orbiculate: Circular, or nearly circular in outline.

Osmosis: The diffusion which proceeds through a semipermeable membrane, separating two miscible solutions, and tending to equalize their concentrations. The movement of solvent or less concentrated solution toward the dense solution while a slower diffusion of the dissolved substance occurs in the opposite direction until both solutions are equal in density.

Osteichthyes: The bony fishes.

Oviparous: Producing eggs which hatch after released from female.

Ovipositor: Organ at hind end of abdomen through which female lays eggs.

Ovoviviparous: Producing eggs which hatch before release from female.

Pancreas: Gland of vertebrates possessing jawbones, situated near the duodenum, into which it discharges certain enzymes for digestive purposes. It also secretes insulin into the blood.

Pectoral: Of, pertaining to, situated or occurring in or on, the breast or chest.

Pectoral fins: The front or upper paired fins behind the head.

Peduncle: As used in this book, the part of the fish where the body blends into the tail of the fish. (*see* Caudal peduncle.)

Pelagic: Of or pertaining to the ocean or open sea.

Peristalsis: Waves of contraction passing along tubular organs particularly intestine, mixing contents and moving them along. Produced by surrounding coats of smooth muscle.

Permeability: Of a membrane, extent to which molecules of given kind or size can pass through it.

Permeable. Said of membrane material that allows passage of molecules.

*p*H: A symbol denoting the negative logarithm of the concentration of the hydrogen ion in gram atoms per liter, used in expressing both acidity and alkalinity. Thus, a *p*H of 6 means a concentration 10^6, or .000001.

Pharynx: Part of vertebrate gut between mouth and esophagus into which open the gill-slits of fish.

Photosynthesis: Formation of carbohydrates in the chlorophyll-containing tissues of plants exposed to light. During this process carbon dioxide and certain nutrients are consumed and carbohydrates are produced.

Plankton: Passively floating or weakly swimming animal and plant life of a body of water. The individual organisms are mostly very small.

Plasma: The fluid in which the blood cells are contained. When all the blood cells are removed from this liquid, it clots as easily as does whole blood.

Posterior: Situated at or relatively nearer to the hind end, that is, usually the end directed backward when the animal is in motion.

Salinity: Amount of dissolved salts in solution.

Semipermeable: Permeable to certain fluid particles, as of water, but not to certain other particles as of dissolved substance which are larger than the particles of water.

Soft dorsal: The posterior part of a dorsal fin composed of soft rays.
Suborbicular: Having somewhat the form of an orb.
Symbiosis (*adj.*, symbiotic): Association of dissimilar organisms to their mutual advantage.

Teleost: A fish of a group (teleostei), the bony fishes.
Toxicity: Quality, state, or degree of being toxic or poisonous; poisonousness.

Vent: The anus.
Ventral: Designating or pertaining to, or situated on or toward, that surface of the body which in man is anterior but in most other animals is the lower surface. Of or pertaining to the belly; abdominal region of the body.
Ventral fins: Paired fins below or behind pectoral fins.
Viviparous: Bringing forth living young.

INDEX